Fashioning Furniture
Beautiful designs that will save you money

Designed, written and illustrated by
John Trigg and David Field
Additional illustrations by Marilyn Day
Photography by Richard Sharpe Studios

ARCO PUBLISHING COMPANY INC.
NEW YORK

Published 1975 by Arco Publishing Company, Inc.
219 Park Avenue South, New York, N.Y. 10003
Designed and produced by Intercontinental Book Productions
Copyright © 1974 by Intercontinental Book Productions
Library of Congress Catalog Card Number 74-19758
ISBN 0-668-03695-8
Printed in Spain

CONTENTS

INTRODUCTION

Nearly everybody at some time or another has tried their hand at painting and decorating their homes, and if honest, has probably been pleasantly surprised at the professional appearance of the results. Unfortunately, however, confidence thus gained is seldom turned to the even more beneficial pursuit of making furniture for the home. This is viewed as being altogether too difficult, challenging and 'way beyond my capabilities'!

With a series of immaculately designed furniture projects, this book sets out to prove that these maxims are not true. The projects themselves vary from the very simple, taking only a few hours to make, to the more complicated, which may take several days to complete, and they have been designed to give a range that complements every part of the home. The making of each is explained in step-by-step stages with clear explicit instructions that are coupled directly with informative, diagrammatic illustrations.

The projects are not always necessarily constructed in the simplest manner. Instead emphasis has been directed in such a way that those who tackle them will be introduced to basic woodworking techniques to a point that will allow them to cope with most household jobs and further furniture making with sure and happy confidence. The rewards from this are many-fold. There's the obvious saving of cost. Raw materials are expensive, but specialist designed furniture, such as that found in this book retails for astronomical figures. There's the satisfactory knowledge that you have broken away from the current trend, in which people are becoming increasingly less self-sufficient, content to call in a 'specialist' to perform even the simplest woodworking tasks around the house and happy to meet any needs by expensive purchase of commercial items. Very importantly, there's the therapeutic pleasure of making things for yourself — in creating something useful and pleasant for your home. This book will help you to achieve all this and at the same time, through its superb design, it offers some original and exciting solutions to domestic furniture problems.

ON USING THIS BOOK

The layout of each project consists of a photograph or drawing of the finished article in situ, underneath which is a list of materials and tools needed for making it. The list of materials can be taken directly to your local supplier and he will prepare the materials to your requirements. Opposite this is an exploded perspective drawing giving material dimensions and showing how all components come together. This is followed by illustration boxes with explicit captions of each stage in the making process.

Check carefully through the tools and special requirements *before* starting a new project to make sure you have all you need, and read through the illustration boxes too so that you are aware of all the processes required and familiar with the project before you start to tackle it. Allow yourself as much time as possible each time you start or return to the making.

Preceding the projects is a section with photographs and explanations of some of the more unusual tools needed. If you have done any woodworking, however elementary, you will probably have most of these, as there is nothing too specialist. There is also a section on some handy hints and technical points, including information on basic materials. We would advise you to read all this carefully before beginning and then refer to it as and when you need to at later stages.

The lumber sizes given in the materials lists should be taken as being the actual sizes needed for each project *after* planing, so, in all cases you should buy the next size larger. For example, if a piece of softwood $\frac{3}{4}$'' x $5\frac{1}{4}$'' is quoted as being required, buy a piece 1'' x 6'' and plane it to the specification given.

Tools You Will Need

1. Adjustable Bevel: Can be set to the required angle.
2. Marking and Mortise Gauge Combined: Arranging depths and marking out a variety of joints.
3. Try-square: Preferably a 12″ blade. Used for marking out joints and testing for squareness.
4. Retractable Tape Measure: Ideal for accurate, measurements and easily stored.

1. Smoothing Plane: Cleaning up and general benchwork.
2. Jack Plane: General benchwork and planing large panels square.
3. Spokeshave: Trimming shaped edges.

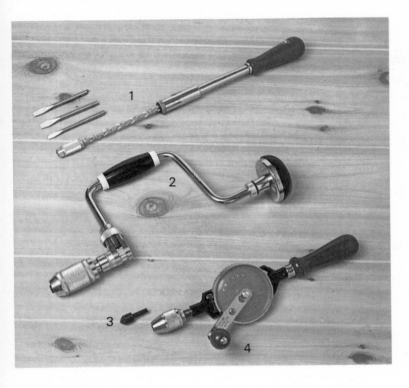

1. Screwdriver: It is advisable to use the ratchet type as shown here as this makes for ease of working.
2. Brace: For drilling dowel holes.
3. Countersink: Used in a wheelbrace for drilling out holes to set screws below surface.
4. Wheelbrace: For drilling holes 1/16th inch diameter to 5/16th inch diameter.

1. Nail Punch: For punching nail heads below surface.
2. Warrington Hammer: Useful weight about 11 oz. General usage.
3. Mallet: For use with chisels in joint cutting.

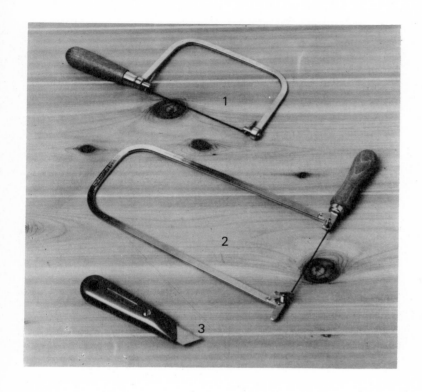

1. Fret Saw: Used for cutting shapes in thin ply.
2. Coping Saw: Very fine blade for cutting out shapes.
3. Knife: Handy for cutting through veneer and soft wood.

1. Cork Sanding Block: Used for wrapping sandpaper around to sand down work.
2. Auger Bit: For deep clean boring such as doweling.
3. Straight-sided Bit. Bores smooth sided holes — used in brace.

1. Back Saw: General bench work and joint cutting.
2. Panel Saw: For cutting large boards into panel sizes.
3. Pad Saw: Handy for cutting out internal shapes.

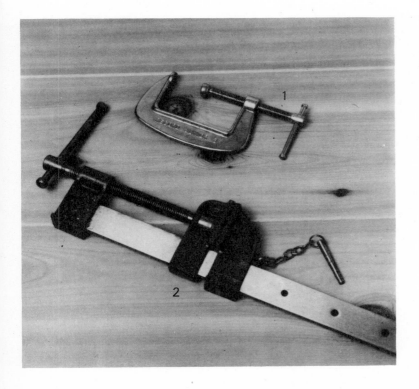

1. G Cramp: Gluing and cramping smaller sections of wood together.
2. Sash Cramp: For cramping up frames and carcasses.

Workbench

A workbench is indispensible if you want firstclass results with the projects in this book. The one shown here has a wood-working vise and bench stop which will accommodate most lumber sections and board sizes while they are being worked. It has been designed with slot-in leg frames, which pack away within the thickness of the top, allowing easy storage.

MATERIALS (in inches)					TOOLS	OTHER REQUIREMENTS
no. off	l.	w.	th.	description		
4	30	$2\frac{3}{4}$	$2\frac{3}{4}$	legs	marking gauge	woodworking adhesive
4	26	$3\frac{3}{4}$	$\frac{3}{4}$	leg frame rails	try-square	matte polyurethane varnish
1	56	$7\frac{1}{2}$	$1\frac{3}{4}$	back rail	back saw	fine sandpaper
1	56	$5\frac{3}{4}$	$1\frac{3}{4}$	front rail	smoothing plane	2 in. No. 10 countersunk woodscrews (18)
1	80	$5\frac{3}{4}$	$\frac{3}{4}$	top frame rails	wheelbrace and drill bits	$2\frac{1}{2}$ in. No. 10 countersunk woodscrews (24)
1	48	$1\frac{3}{4}$	$1\frac{3}{4}$	blocks	pad saw	54 in. mild steel 1 in. x 1 in. angle section
3	56	$5\frac{3}{4}$	$1\frac{3}{4}$	top boards	screwdriver	7 in. woodworking vise
1	30	$\frac{1}{2}$	dia.	dowel	$\frac{3}{4}$ in. beveled edged chisel	Package of 1 in. panel pins
1	56	9	$\frac{3}{4}$	top board	mallet	$\frac{3}{4}$ in. No. 8 countersunk woodscrews (12)
2	56	1	1	90° triangle		2 in. x $\frac{1}{4}$ in. dia. coach bolt and wing nut (1)
1	24	$3\frac{3}{4}$	$2\frac{3}{4}$	vice mount		

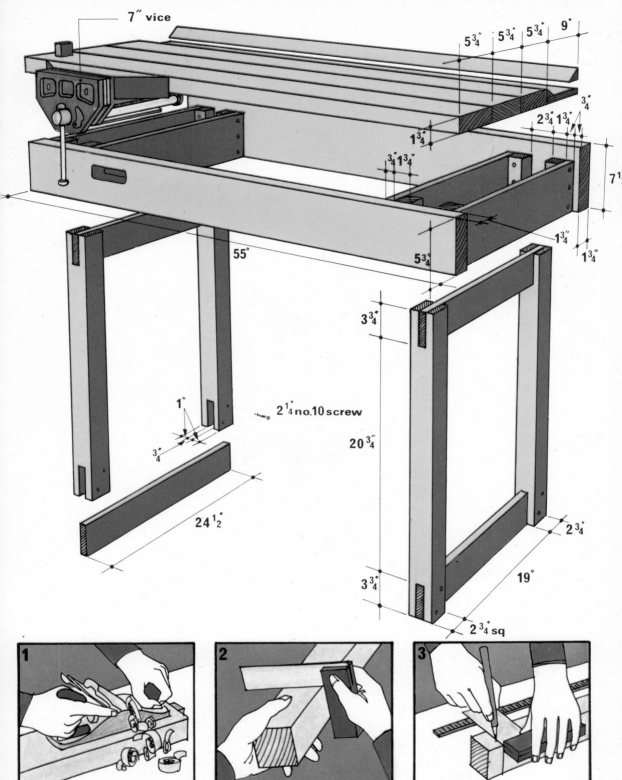

7″ vice

$5\frac{3}{4}''$ $5\frac{3}{4}''$ $5\frac{3}{4}''$ 9″

$\frac{3}{4}''$

$2\frac{3}{4}''$ $1\frac{3}{4}''$

$1\frac{3}{4}''$

$\frac{3}{4}''$ $1\frac{3}{4}''$

$7\frac{1}{2}$

55″

$5\frac{3}{4}$

$1\frac{3}{4}''$

$1\frac{3}{4}''$

$3\frac{3}{4}''$

1″

$2\frac{1}{4}''$ no.10 screw

$\frac{3}{4}''$

$20\frac{3}{4}''$

$24\frac{1}{2}''$

$2\frac{3}{4}''$

$3\frac{3}{4}''$

19″

$2\frac{3}{4}''$ sq

1 Plane all wood to size.

2 Check for squareness, using a try-square.

3 Mark off required lengths, using a try-square and pencil, and cut to the scribed line, using a back saw.

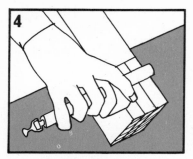

4 Mark out bridal joints for leg frames, using a marking gauge.

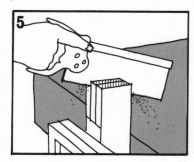

5 Using a back saw, cut down to the scribed line. Chisel out the center section and smooth sides of the cut-out.

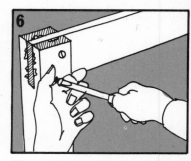

6 Glue and screw the top and base rails to the uprights. Use 2 in. No. 10 woodscrews.

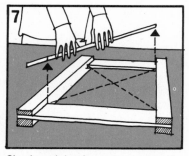

7 Check each leg frame for squareness by applying the 'diagonal test,' using a thin wooden lath.

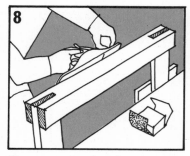

8 Clean up the leg frames using smoothing plane and a fine sandpaper.

9 Construct the four under-rails by gluing the screwing blocks to each end. Use 2 in. No. 10 woodscrews.

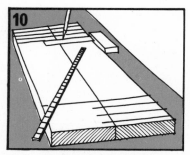

10 Mark out the two pieces of wood forming the front and back overhangs in readiness to take under-rails.

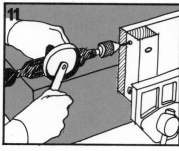

11 Hold the under-rails and drill the end blocks to take no. 10 woodscrews.

12 Glue and screw under-rails to front and rear overhangs using $2\frac{1}{2}$ in. No. 10 woodscrews. Dimension * must be accurate.

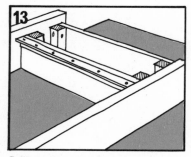

13 Drill and screw into position the metal angle strips using $\frac{3}{4}$ in. No. 8 woodscrews.

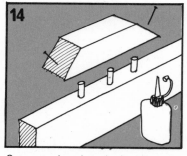

14 Cut out, dowel and glue the vise mounting into position.

15 Mark out and cut aperture to take vise mechanism. Drill the corners and cut around the scribed line with a pad saw.

16

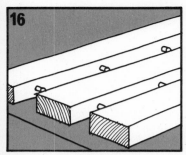

Drill and dowel the pieces of wood which form the bench top surface. No glue is required.

17

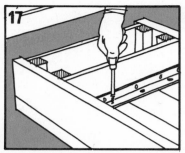

Use $\frac{3}{4}$ in. No. 8 woodscrews to screw the top to the under-frame through the metal angle strips.

18

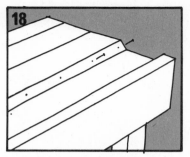

Using panel pins, fix the triangular strips into position to complete the tool-well.

19

Mark out and mortise the 'Bench Stop' hole using $\frac{3}{4}$ in. bevel edged chisel and mallet.

20

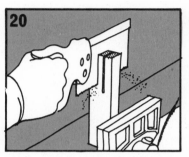

Mark out and cut the bench stop to length. Saw out slot wide enough to slide over the coach bolt.

21

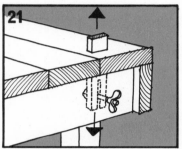

Position bench stop and mark position for coach bolt. Drill $\frac{1}{4}$ in. hole and fix. Check action of bench stop.

22

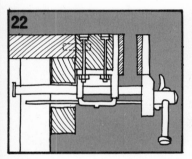

Fix the vise to the bench mounting, following the manufacturer's instructions.

23

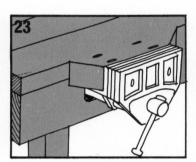

Check the action of the vise. Plug the fixing holes on the bench surface, using $\frac{1}{2}$ in. beech dowels.

26

24

Sand down all surfaces then apply a coat of polyurethane varnish or rub in several coats of linseed oil.

25

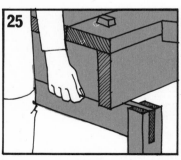

The bench can be erected by slotting the leg frames between the under-rail bolt.

When not in use, the leg frames can be stored underneath the bench top.

Coffee Table

An occasional table of simple construction using the qualities of dark and light colored lumber for visual effect. It is designed to be made easily using only a few basic tools. The result is an original table of robust structure for use in living room or sitting areas of the home.

MATERIALS (in inches)					TOOLS	OTHER REQUIREMENTS
no. off	l.	w.	th.	description		
16	11	$1\frac{5}{8}$	$1\frac{5}{8}$	legs hardwood	try-square	medium and fine sandpaper
4	17	$1\frac{5}{8}$	$1\frac{5}{8}$	rails hardwood	back saw	woodworking adhesive
4	24	$1\frac{5}{8}$	$\frac{1}{2}$	rails hardwood	marking gauge	matte polyurethane varnish
8	6	$1\frac{5}{8}$	$\frac{1}{2}$	feet hardwood	$\frac{1}{2}$ in. & 1 in. beveled edge chisels	1 in. paintbrush
1	$20\frac{1}{2}$	$20\frac{1}{2}$	$\frac{5}{8}$	top plywood	wheelbrace and drill bits	string
1	16	—	$\frac{3}{8}$	beech dowel	brace and $\frac{3}{8}$ in. auger bit	$1\frac{1}{4}$ in. No. 8 countersunk
					pincers	woodscrews (24)
					screwdriver	pkg. of panel pins
					hammer	furniture wax
					bench hook	
					countersink	
					G-cramps	

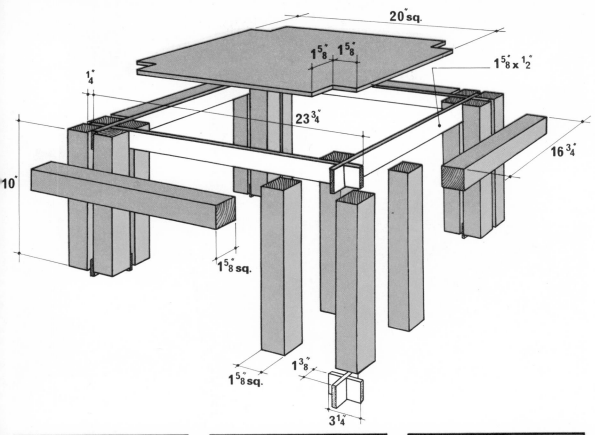

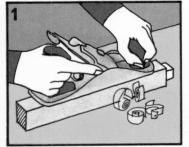

1 Set a smoothing plane to a fine cut and plane all components square.

2 Test ends for squareness. Where necessary mark square ends.

3 Cut ends square with a back saw, using a bench hook to hold wood against. Cut waste side of line.

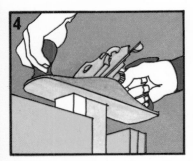

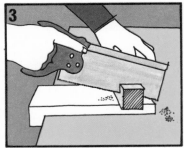

4 Cramp component in vise with a piece of waste wood. This prevents splitting out of end grain. Plane ends square.

5 Place square ends together and mark out lengths of all elements.

6 Using a square, mark out positions of halving joints on side rails. Mark in pairs and number for reference.

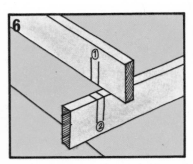

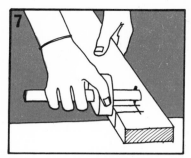

Set a marking gauge to half the depth of rail and gauge depth of cut as illustrated.

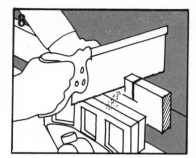

Cramp rail firmly in vise and cut down to gauge line with a back saw. Do not overcut as this will weaken joint.

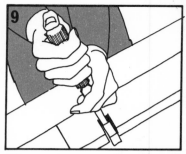

Chip out the waste piece of wood with a $\frac{1}{2}$ in. bevel chisel, paring down to the gauge line.

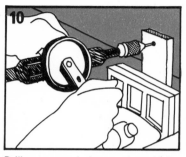

Drill out screw holes to take a $1\frac{1}{4}$ in. No. 8 steel countersunk screw.

Countersink all holes so that the screw head lies just below the wood surface in all cases.

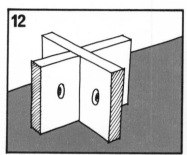

The four-leg combination has a small unit as shown tying them at the base. The halving joint for this is not glued.

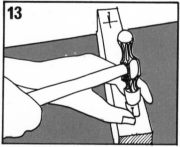

Mark dowel positions on side rails and tap in panel pins to a depth of $\frac{1}{4}$ in.

Pinch off the heads of the pins as illustrated, leaving a sharp metal protrusion of $\frac{1}{8}$ in.

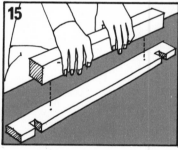

Mark out dowel positions on corresponding side rails by pressing rails together. Leave pin hole impressions.

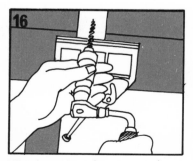

With a brace and $\frac{3}{8}$ in. auger, drill out all dowel holes.

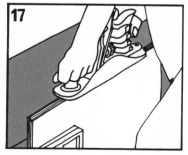

Cut top to size and plane edges square.

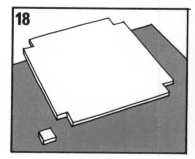

Cut out corner pieces $1\frac{5}{8} \times 1\frac{5}{8}$ in. to length with a back saw and bench hook.

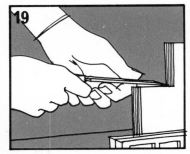

19 Clean off saw cut marks with a 1 in. bevel chisel.

20 Fit halving joints together but do not glue. Screw and glue inside legs to side rails.

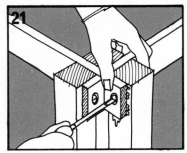

21 Glue and screw outside legs into position both to side rails and to small cross unit at the base of the legs.

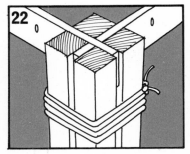

22 Glue outside corner legs into position. Tie up the four-leg combination tightly with string and allow glue to set.

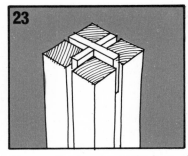

23 The small cross unit at the base of the leg protrudes $\frac{1}{4}$ in. giving the leg proper clearance above ground level.

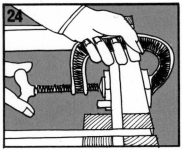

24 Cramp and glue side rails together. Glue $\frac{3}{8}$ in. dowels into place so that $\frac{1}{2}$ in. protrudes to provide support for the top.

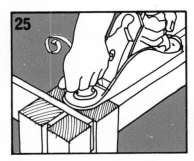

25 Set smoothing plane to a fine cut and clean rails down to tops of legs. Take care not to split out the end grain.

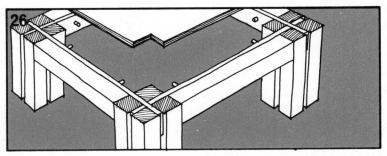

26 Fit the top into position. If necessary, improve fit by shaving slightly with the smoothing plane. Make sure that it sits evenly on all the dowels. If necessary sand dowels down to the correct level.

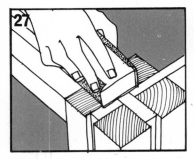

27 Using a medium fine sandpaper, sand down the table, cleaning off all sharp arrises. Finish with a very fine sandpaper.

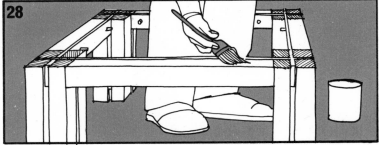

28 Coat all wood with polyurethane clear matte varnish. When dry rub down with fine sandpaper. Coat again with polyurethane and finish with fine sandpaper that has first been smeared with white wax. Leave to dry and then rub off with a dry cloth.

Column Display Unit

A column of identical boxes made of standard deal for the storage and display of small objects, special possessions, books and small plants. The unit consists of a base on to which the boxes are mounted, and the number of boxes can vary according to the height of column required.

MATERIALS (in inches)					TOOLS	OTHER REQUIREMENTS
no. off	l.	w.	th.	description		
4	48	$9\frac{3}{4}$	$\frac{3}{4}$	boxes	marking gauge	woodworking adhesive
3	36	$\frac{1}{4}$	dia.	dowel	wheelbrace and $\frac{1}{4}$ in. drill bit	polyurethane paint
1	20	20	$\frac{3}{4}$	base	smoothing plane	fine sandpaper
					back saw	
					bench hook	
					cork sanding block	

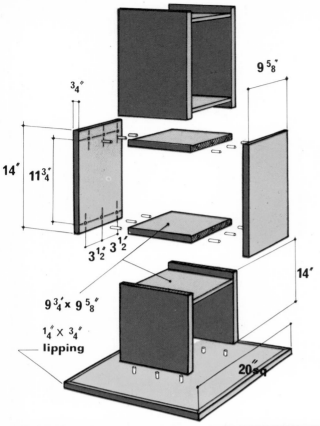

$9\frac{5}{8}''$

$\frac{3}{4}''$

$14''$ $11\frac{3}{4}''$

$3\frac{1}{2}''$ $3\frac{1}{2}''$

$9\frac{3}{4}'' \times 9\frac{5}{8}''$

$\frac{1}{4}'' \times \frac{3}{4}''$
lipping

$14''$

$20''$sq

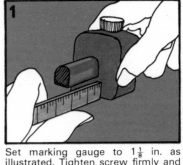

Set marking gauge to $1\frac{1}{8}$ in. as illustrated. Tighten screw firmly and re-check setting.

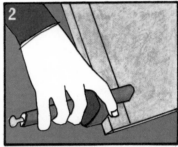

After cutting lumber to size, scribe a line down each end of the box sides to mark the position of the dowels.

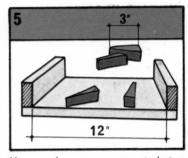

Mark out spacing of the dowel holes on the scribed line using a center punch.

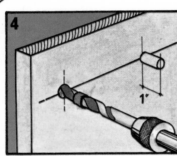

Drill holes in top and base to a depth of $\frac{1}{2}$ in. dowels $1\frac{1}{2}$ in. long.

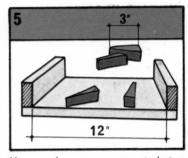

Use sash cramps or make a cramping board and wedges to hold the job while glue sets.

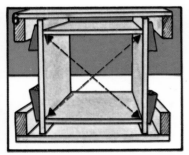

Apply glue and place job in cramping board. Drive in wedges. Check for squareness using the 'diagonal test'.

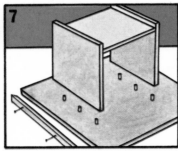

The assembly of the base relies on the same dowel joints used on the boxes.

Paint the finished boxes with matte polyurethane paint, using colors of your own choice.

Bookends

The bookends are two identical objects used to hold books on a desk, sideboard or open-ended shelving. They consist of a wooden sandwich made from two different colored woods, on to which is screwed a metal plate. Simplicity and unobtrusiveness make them ideal for use with any books or furniture styles.

MATERIALS (in inches)					TOOLS	OTHER REQUIREMENTS
no. off	l.	w.	th.	description		
4	7½	4½	½	dark wood	back saw smoothing plane cork sanding block wheelbrace and drill bits file screwdriver bench hook	woodworking adhesive matte polyurethane varnish 1 in. No. 4 brass woodscrews (4) fine sandpaper 2 in. paint brush furniture wax
2	7½	4½	½	light wood		
2	3	3	—	16 gauge duraluminum		

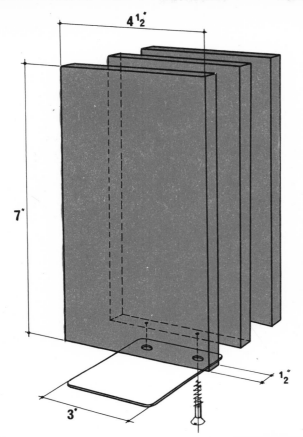

4½"

7"

3'

½"

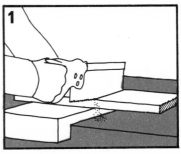

Cut the pieces of wood to size, using a back saw and bench hook.

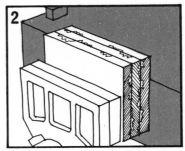

Glue the pieces together and cramp in a vise or place under heavy weights. Remove all surplus glue.

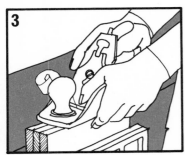

Clean up edges by planing from each end towards the center. This avoids splitting the wood at the ends.

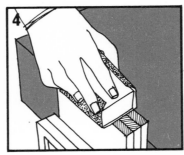

Using fine sandpaper and a cork sanding block, clean up all edges.

Place metal plate against waste wood in the vise. Drill and countersink fixing holes to take No. 4 woodscrews.

Round off the corners of the metal plates by placing them in the vise and using a file.

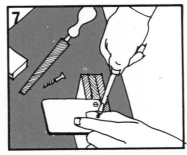

Fix the metal plates to the wood using No. 4 woodscrews.

Coat the wood with polyurethane varnish and, when dry, rub furniture wax over surface.

Easy Chair

The chair body, made from thin plywood stressed over shaped plywood side panels, will be strong, easy to make and inexpensive. A careful choice of paint color and cushion fabric will allow it to blend nicly into most domestic areas, living room, workroom, den, etc.

MATERIALS (in inches)					TOOLS	OTHER REQUIREMENTS
no. off	l.	w.	th.	description		
2	18	$21\frac{1}{2}$	$\frac{3}{4}$	sides	fret saw	$2\frac{1}{2}$ sq. yds. material
1	24	48	$\frac{3}{16}$	back and seat	pad saw	48 in. Velcro tape
1	24	36	$\frac{3}{16}$	back	spokeshave	woodworking adhesive
1	24	18	$\frac{3}{16}$	front	smoothing plane	contact adhesive
1	24	20	$\frac{1}{2}$	infil pieces	back saw	fine sandpaper
1	72	$2\frac{3}{4}$	$\frac{3}{4}$	softwood rails	hammer	polyurethane paint
2	46	24	2	medium and soft foam	punch	pkg. of panel pins
					trysquare	standard wood filler
					sewing machine	2 in. paint brush
					bench hook	
					wheelbrace and drill bits	
					cork sanding block	

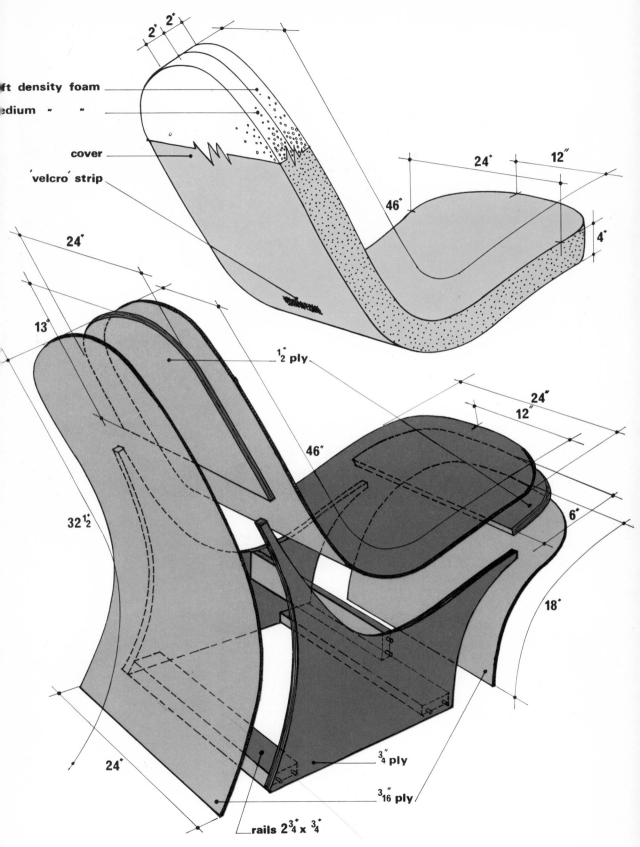

ft density foam

edium ~ ~

cover

'velcro' strip

2" 2"

24" 12"

46"

4"

24"

13"

$\frac{1}{2}$" ply

46"

24"

12"

6"

32 $\frac{1}{2}$"

18"

24"

$\frac{3}{4}$" ply

$\frac{3}{16}$" ply

rails 2 $\frac{3}{4}$" x $\frac{3}{4}$"

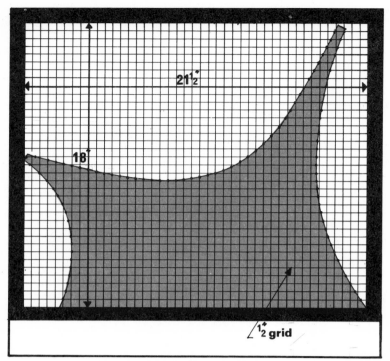

21 1/2"

18"

1/2" grid

Draw 1/2 in. grid on one plywood side panel. Use grid to plot curves. Intersection points should match drawing.

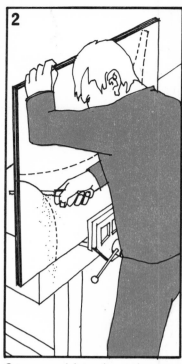

2

Cramp panel into vise and cut out the shape, using a pad saw. Cut waste side of line, leaving a little to clean off.

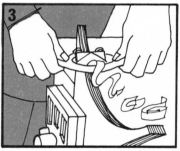

3

Spokeshave down to the line. This side panel can be used as a template to mark out the neighboring panel.

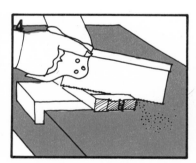

4

Cut cross rails to length using a back saw and a bench hook to hold firmly.

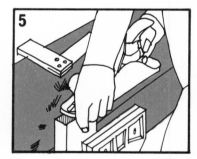

5

Plane ends square with a smoothing plane, working from both directions to avoid splitting the end grain.

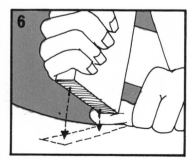

6

Mark dowel positions with panel pins. Clip off heads and impress on side panels. Drill out and number the joints.

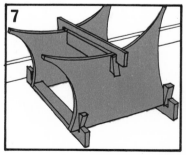

7

Make up 3 simple cramps with wedges as shown and glue up main frame. Check all joints with try-square.

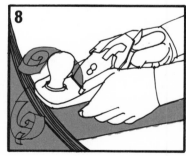

8

Clean down rails with a smoothing plane, bringing them into alignment with outside curves.

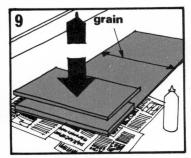

9 grain

Glue ½ in. ply infill to back. The grain on outer veneer of the job must run at right angles to grain on back.

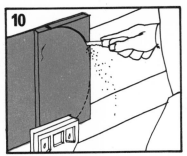

10

Radius and cut out with a pad saw, but do not clean down to the line.

11

Glue and pin the plywood back and seat form to main chair frame. Punch pin heads just below the surface.

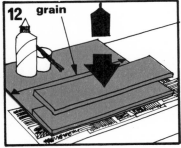

12 grain

Glue ½ in. ply infill to front panel.

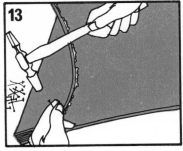

13

Pin and glue to front of main chair frame. Angle pins to hold the ply form firmly in position.

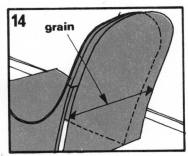

14 grain

Radius the ply back and glue and pin into position.

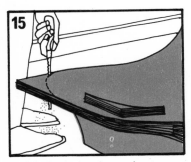

15

Radius the front edge and cut away waste wood with a pad saw.

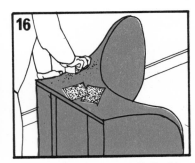

16

All nail holes should be filled with a wood filler and whole chair well sanded to receive a painted finish.

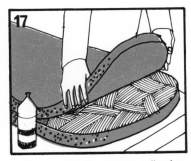

17

Using standard contact adhesive, glue together medium and soft density foam. Keep 2 sheets flat when joining them.

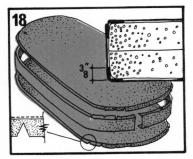

18

3⅜"

Cut fabric cover as shown and stitch pieces together. Leave an opening so the foam can be inserted.

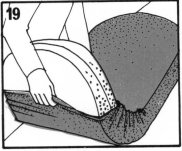

19

Pull cover over foam and slipstitch opening. Stitch on corresponding 'Velcro' strips on inside face.

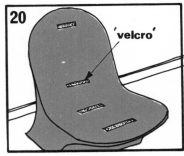

20 'velcro'

Paint chair to required finish and glue on 'Velcro' strips with a contact adhesive.

Storage Unit

A system of boxes, identical in width and made in two depths, which provides storage for books and records. The boxes, painted the same or two different colors, can be linked in a large number of variations extending horizontally or vertically. Care must be taken when drilling the holes for the linking rods, otherwise alignment may prove difficult.

MATERIALS (in inches)					TOOLS	OTHER REQUIREMENTS
no. off	l.	w.	th.	description		

16	21½	14	¾	sides	try-square
					back saw
					marking gauge
					wheelbrace and drill bits
					screwdriver
					brace and straight-sided bit
					punch
					smoothing plane
					bench hook
					cork sanding block
						fine sandpaper
						1 in. No. 8 countersunk
						  woodscrews (100)
						1¼ in. No. 8 countersunk
						  woodscrews (100)
						1½ in. oval nails (½ lb.)
						woodworking adhesive
						2 in. paintbrush
						primer paint
						polyurethane paint
						standard wood filler

16	14	12	¼	panels		
16	14	10½	¼	inside panels		
32	12	2½	¾	timbers		
32	14	2½	¾	timbers		
4	62	1 7/16	dia.	poles		
2	38	1 7/16	dia.	poles		

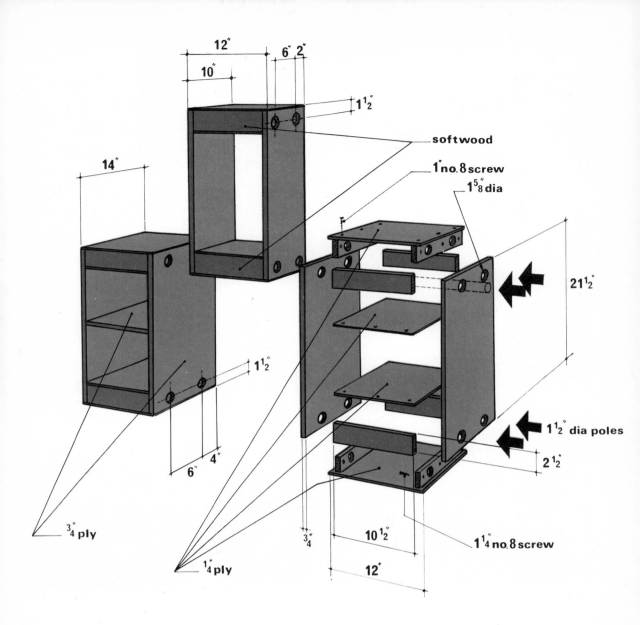

12"
10"
6" 2"
$1\frac{1}{2}$"
14"
softwood
1" no. 8 screw
$1\frac{5}{8}$" dia
$21\frac{1}{2}$"
$1\frac{1}{2}$"
$1\frac{1}{2}$" dia poles
$2\frac{1}{2}$"
$\frac{3}{4}$" ply
6" 4"
$\frac{3}{4}$"
$\frac{1}{4}$" ply
$10\frac{1}{2}$"
$1\frac{1}{4}$" no. 8 screw
12"

1 Check that all components are square and that no serious defects exist in any of the members.

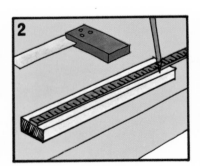

2 Mark out the lengths of all timbers and square off with a try-square.

3 Using bench hook and back saw cut ends. Trim square with smoothing plane. Take care not to split end grain.

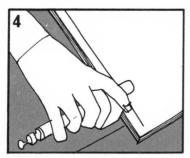

4

Set marking gauge to $\frac{3}{4}$ in. Mark along inside faces of the top and bottom.

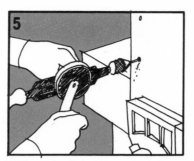

5

With a wheelbrace and bit, drill out positions for No. 8 countersunk woodscrews.

6

Countersink the holes so that the head of the screw sits just below surface of the panel.

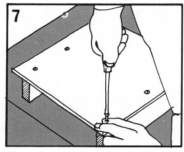

7

Glue and screw timbers into position; use 1 in. woodscrews. Wipe off any surplus glue with a damp cloth.

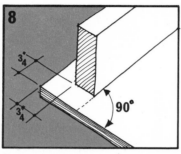

8

The timber should be positioned square to front of panel. This is critical: all boxes must be square to fit together.

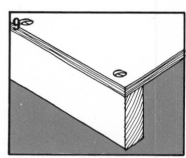

9

Glue and screw inside panels to timbers making sure they are flush along the edge. Use 1 in. woodscrews.

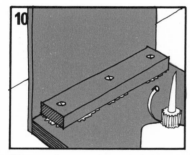

10

Glue and screw top and bottom panels to side panels and wipe off all surplus glue. Use $1\frac{1}{4}$ in. woodscrews.

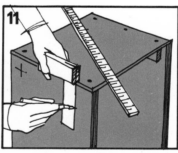

11

Mark out position of the holes for the linking poles.

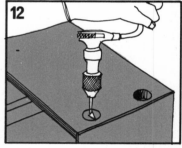

12

Using a brace and straight-sided bit, drill out holes. Hold a block of waste wood against inside face to prevent wood splitting.

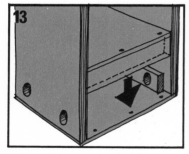

13

Fit top and bottom inside panels to main box frame. You may need to take off a shaving here and there, to get an exact fit.

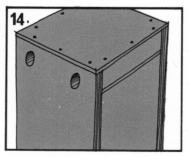

14

Glue the inside panel and screw into position from the outside. Use 1 in. woodscrews.

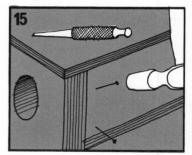

15

Dovetail nail through the front timber into the end of the side timbers and punch nails home.

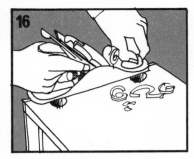

16 Set a smoothing plane to a very fine cut and clean off any protruding edges.

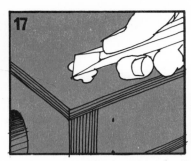

17 Using a standard filler, stop up all screw and nail holes flush with the surface.

18 Sand down whole job, starting with a coarse sandpaper and finishing with a fine one.

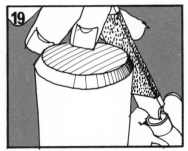

19 Cut all poles to length and bevel edges with sandpaper folded tight around a broad-bladed chisel or cork sanding block.

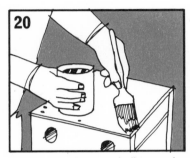

20 Prime all surfaces and allow to dry. Rub down with fine sandpaper and apply first coat.

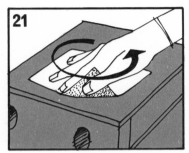

21 Rub down again and apply final topcoat. Use polyurethane paint for durability.

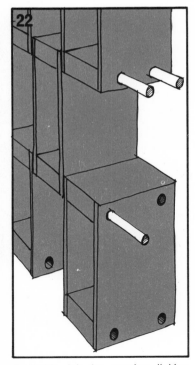

22 Assemble job by passing linking poles through holes. These should not be glued or fixed in any way.

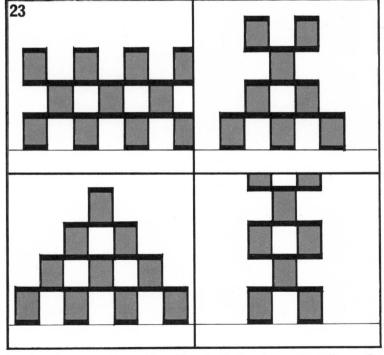

23 A variety of arrangements can be achieved with these boxes, depending on size of room and general layout required.

Magazine Rack

This piece of furniture made of standard deal is designed to store magazines, newspapers, and periodicals, while doubling as a small table. There are no cut joints to worry about since the unit is constructed by gluing, screwing and tacking. Once all holes and gaps are filled and sanded, a paint finish can be applied in a color that suits the room in which it will be used.

no. off	l.	w.	th.	description	TOOLS	OTHER REQUIREMENTS
2	$19\frac{1}{2}$	12	$\frac{3}{8}$	end panels	back saw	woodworking adhesive
2	$17\frac{1}{4}$	12	$\frac{3}{8}$	top	bench hook	2 in. No. 10 countersunk
4	$10\frac{1}{2}$	12	$\frac{3}{8}$	center panels	screwdriver	woodscrews (6)
5	13	$1\frac{3}{4}$	$1\frac{1}{4}$	timbers	smoothing plane	1 in. No. 8 countersunk
5	13	$3\frac{1}{4}$	$1\frac{1}{4}$	lippings	hammer	woodscrews (36)
8	13	$1\frac{1}{4}$	$1\frac{1}{4}$	top timbers	cork sanding block	fine sandpaper
					wheelbrace and drill bits	standard wood filler
					countersink	polyurethane paint
						2 in. paint brush
						pkg. $1\frac{1}{4}$ in. panel pins

The first column group is headed **MATERIALS (in inches)**.

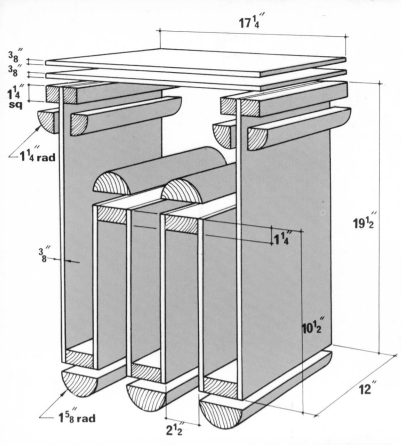

17¼″

$\frac{3}{8}$″
$\frac{3}{8}$″

1¼″ sq

1¼″ rad

$\frac{3}{8}$″

1⅝″ rad

2½″

1¼″

19½″

10½″

12″

Cut solid pieces of wood to length using bench hook and back saw.

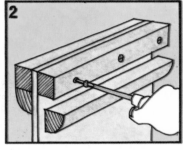

Plane the curved pieces and glue and screw with square blocks into position. Use 2 in. No. 10 woodscrews.

Glue and screw blocks and uprights in the sequence shown.

Plane edge of the boards flush with the surface of the solid blocks.

Glue and tack semi-circular pieces into position. Use 1¼ in. panel pins.

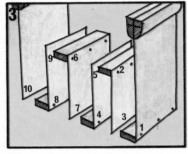

Screw and glue the first top board into position. Use 1 in. No. 8 woodscrews.

Glue the second top board on to the first and cramp or place a heavy weight on the surface.

Fill edges and tack marks. Sand down and paint with 3 coats.

Home Filing Unit

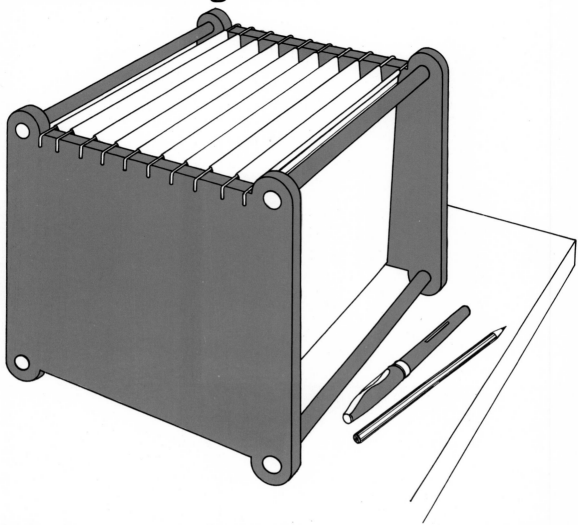

The filing unit is made up of cardboard lengths glued together, folded, and supported on bent wire lengths between two painted plywood sides. The compartments provided allow the filing of invoices, receipts, letters, insurance policies, bank statements, agreements and contracts, etc. Tabs, which fix to the cardboard, allowing quick referencing, can be bought from office supply stores.

MATERIALS (in inches)					TOOLS	OTHER REQUIREMENTS
no. off	l.	w.	th.	description		
2	12	12	$\frac{1}{2}$	plywood sides	fret/coping saw	fine sandpaper
4	13		$\frac{3}{4}$ dia.	dowel	brace & bit	paint
4	2		$\frac{1}{4}$ dia.	dowel	pliers	cardboard ($11\frac{3}{4}$ in. wide)
					smoothing plane	16 gauge wire (5 yds)
					compass	circular self-adhesive labels
					scissors	woodworking adhesive
					wheelbrace & drill bits	contact adhesive

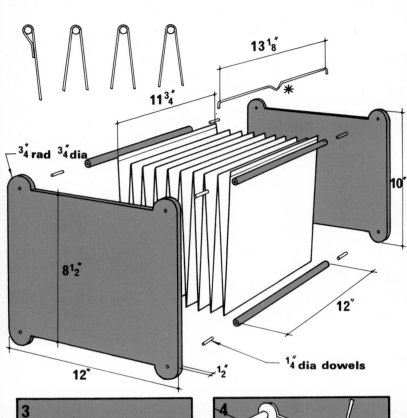

13 $\frac{1}{8}$"

11 $\frac{3}{4}$"

$\frac{3}{4}$" rad $\frac{3}{4}$" dia

10"

8 $\frac{1}{2}$"

12"

12"

$\frac{1}{2}$"

$\frac{1}{4}$" dia dowels

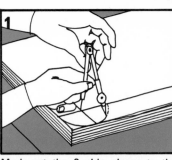

1

Mark out the 2 side pieces to the correct dimensions. Use compass to mark the radii at the corners.

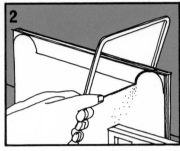

2

Using the coping saw, cut to the scribed lines. Plane any rough edges and surfaces and then sand down.

3

1 $\frac{3}{4}$"

Drill the holes to take the cross dowels.

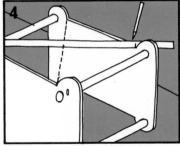

4

Assemble box, checking for squareness. Paint box and fix self adhesive labels over dowels.

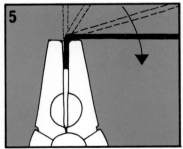

5

Cut 10 pieces of wire approx 18 in. long. Bend the kink with pliers. Bend ends to fit. Snip off surplus wire.

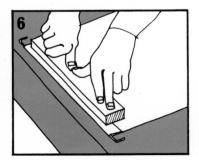

6

Glue the cardboard end pieces over the wire, using contact adhesive.

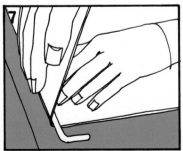

7

Fold the cardboard over the wire pieces after marking out position of the crease.

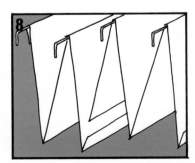

8

Join the pieces of cardboard together on the bottom fold, again using contact adhesive.

Corner Cabinet

A cabinet to fit into corner spaces in living rooms and used for storage of china, glassware or objects you want to protect from dust. It is made of simple plywood or blockboard construction. The inside can be covered in colored felt, as described in the instruction boxes, or painted if used for drinks storage.

MATERIALS (in inches)				TOOLS	OTHER REQUIREMENTS
no. off	l.	w.	th.	description		

no. off	l.	w.	th.	description
2	33	17	$\frac{3}{4}$	plywood sides
2	17	17	$\frac{3}{4}$	plywood shelves
2	33	10	$\frac{1}{2}$	plywood doors
2	33	$\frac{3}{4}$	$\frac{3}{4}$	side lippings
4	33	$1\frac{1}{2}$	$\frac{1}{2}$	door lippings
4	33	10	$\frac{1}{16}$	formica laminate
1	48		$\frac{1}{4}$ dia.	dowel

TOOLS

rip saw
back saw
smoothing plane
wheelbrace and drill bits
masonry drill bit
screwdriver
try-square
countersink
pliers
hammer
scissors
adjustable bevel
marking gauge
craft knife

OTHER REQUIREMENTS

fine sandpaper
woodworking adhesive
contact adhesive
adhesive spreader
felt
polyurethane paint
magnetic catches (2)
$2\frac{1}{2}$ in. brass butt hinges (4)
pkg. panel pins
$1\frac{1}{4}$ in. No. 8 countersunk woodscrews (36)
$2\frac{1}{2}$ in. No. 10 countersunk woodscrews (6)
rawl plugs (6)
colored felt (2 yds.)

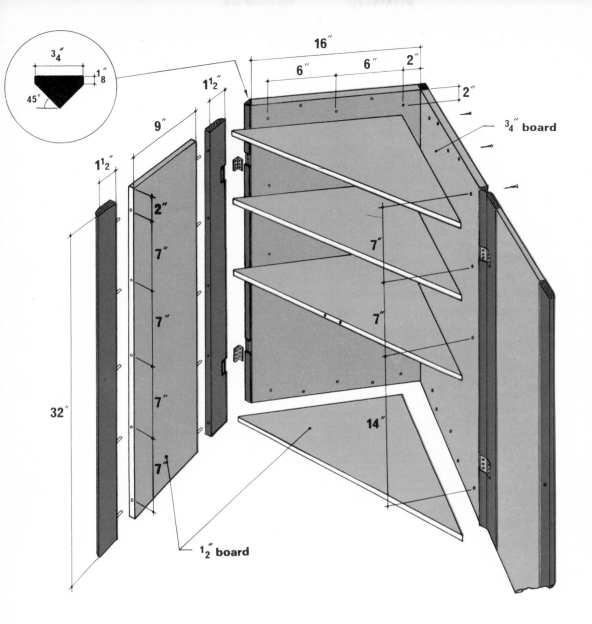

$\frac{3}{4}''$

$\frac{1}{8}''$

45°

16″

6″

6″

2″

2″

$\frac{3}{4}''$ board

$1\frac{1}{2}''$

9″

$1\frac{1}{2}''$

2″

7″

7″

7″

7″

7″

7″

7″

32″

14″

$\frac{1}{2}''$ board

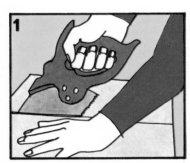

1 Cut all panels to size with a saw.

2 Plane all panels square and to exact dimensions. Check for squareness using try-square.

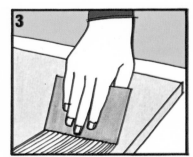

3 Spread doors and plastic laminate with contact adhesive and leave for 15 minutes. (Spreader often supplied with glue.)

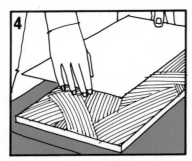

4 Press 2 surfaces firmly together, making sure edges align on impact. Use smoothing plane to level top and bottom.

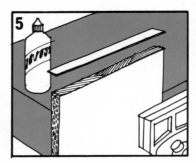

5 The same process is applied when gluing on the edging strips at the top and bottom of the door panel.

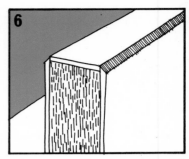

6 Using a smoothing plane, put a 45° chamfer along each edge.

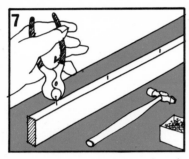

7 Mark out dowel positions and tap in panel pins. Clip off nail heads with pliers leaving $\frac{1}{8}$ in. protrusion.

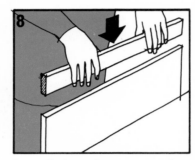

8 Press lippings down on to door panel, leaving pin-marks. Drill $\frac{1}{4}$ in. dowel holes 1 in. deep.

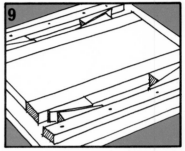

9 Make up a simple cramping board with wedges and glue on lippings. Wipe off any surplus glue with damp cloth.

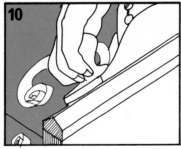

10 Pin and glue lippings on to carcass panels and angle with a plane. Set an adjustable bevel to 45° to check angle.

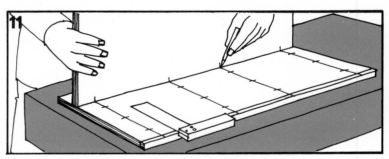

11 Mark out shelf positions on main carcass sides, measuring on one and then scribing on to the other as shown.

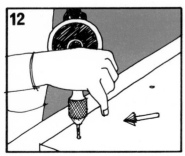

12 Drill out holes to take $1\frac{1}{4}$ in. No. 8 woodscrews and countersink heads just below the surface.

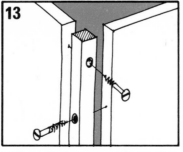

13 Drill out back corner piece at 3 in. intervals, alternating at 90° to each other.

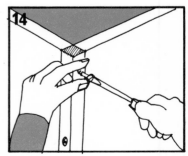

14 Screw and glue the 2 cabinet sides together. Check that they are square before allowing glue to set.

15 Cut plywood shelves to size. Clean up the edges with a smoothing plane; glue and screw in place.

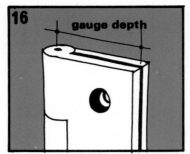

16 Set marking gauge to depth shown. The length of hinges should be 2½ in., preferably the solid drawn brass type.

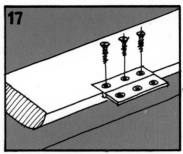

17 Mark out position of hinges on both doors. Gauge in width of hinge. Fit hinge flush with surface of lipping.

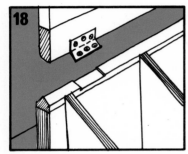

18 Offer the door up to the main cabinet and mark off position of hinge. Fit hinge flush with surface of the lipping.

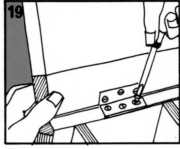

19 Screw into position with two screws first and then check that door swings correctly; if so, add third and final screw.

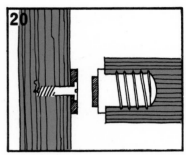

20 Fit magnetic catch and screw on corresponding plate to doors, ensuring that the 2 are accurately aligned.

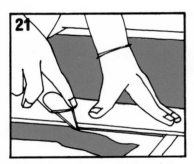

21 Use a piece of waste chipboard as a cutting board. Cut felt to size, using a sharp craft knife and metal ruler.

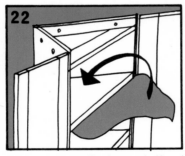

22 Apply contact adhesive to shelf and felt surfaces (leave for 15 minutes), then press firmly into position.

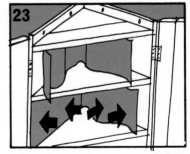

23 Felt will stretch as pressed into position and will need trimming to fit. Use a sharp craft knife and metal ruler.

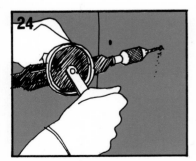

24 Mark cabinet position on wall. Drill out screw hole positions to a depth of 2 in. with a wheelbrace and No. 10 masonry bit.

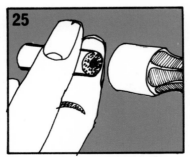

25 Hammer 2 in. rawl plugs into position. These should fit tightly to ensure firm fixing for the cabinet.

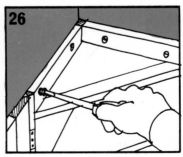

26 Support the cabinet in position and screw home 2½ in. No. 10 steel countersunk woodscrews.

Dining Room Chair

The dining chair relates visually to the table, although it may be used with other furniture. It is of simple dowel construction and can be made from any hardwood. The seat and back can be upholstered simply with a variety of fabrics.

no. off	l.	w.	th.	description	TOOLS	OTHER REQUIREMENTS
2	28	$2\frac{1}{4}$	$\frac{3}{4}$	back legs	trysquare	woodworking adhesive
1	17	$2\frac{1}{4}$	$\frac{3}{4}$	front legs	back saw	contact adhesive
3	12	$2\frac{1}{4}$	$\frac{3}{4}$	rails	bench hook	fine sandpaper
2	16	$2\frac{1}{4}$	$\frac{3}{4}$	rails	wheelbrace and drill bits	pkg. $\frac{3}{8}$ in. tacks
1	$19\frac{3}{4}$	$16\frac{1}{2}$	$\frac{1}{2}$	ply seat	countersink	matte polyurethane varnish
1	$19\frac{3}{4}$	$16\frac{1}{2}$	1	heavy density foam	brace	2 in. No. 10 countersunk
1	11	8	1	heavy density foam	smoothing plane	woodscrews (6)
					sash cramps	pkg. panel pins
					hammer	upholstery material 26 in. × 23 in.
					rasp	17 in. × 14 in.
					screwdriver	same amount of calico
					$\frac{1}{4}$ in. auger bit	
					pliers	
					sewing machine	
					cork sanding block	

Table header: MATERIALS (in inches)

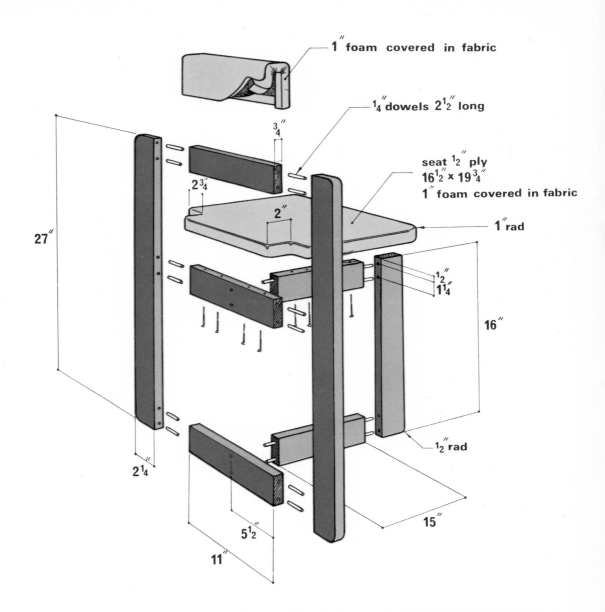

1″ foam covered in fabric

$\frac{1}{4}$″ dowels $2\frac{1}{2}$″ long

seat $\frac{1}{2}$″ ply
$16\frac{1}{2}$″ x $19\frac{3}{4}$″
1″ foam covered in fabric

1″ rad

$\frac{3}{4}$″

$2\frac{3}{4}$″

2″

27″

$\frac{1}{2}$″
$1\frac{1}{4}$″

16″

$2\frac{1}{4}$″

$\frac{1}{2}$″ rad

$5\frac{1}{2}$″

15″

11″

1

Mark a square end on each piece of wood using a trysquare

2

Cut ends square with back saw, holding wood firm against a bench hook.

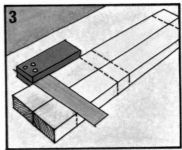

3

Cut all members to length and mark out position of joints with a trysquare.

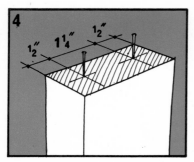

4

Mark out position of dowels as illustrated and tap in panel pins.

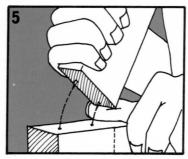

5

Cut heads off the pins with pliers and press rail into position on leg, leaving an impression of the pin holes.

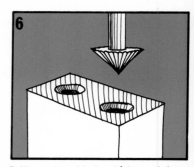

6

Drill out dowel holes $1\frac{1}{4}$ in. and then countersink to provide a lead-in for the dowel.

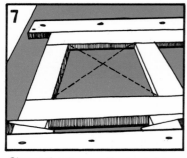

7

Glue and cramp up the back frame, using blocks and wedges, and allow to set. Check for squareness using the 'diagonal test.'

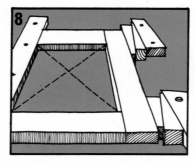

8

Glue and cramp up the front frame in the same manner. Again check for squareness.

9

Cramp frame firmly in the vise and clean down joints with a smoothing plane.

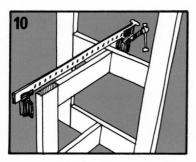

10

Cramp the 2 frames together, making sure you have a perfect right angle joint between them. Use sash cramps.

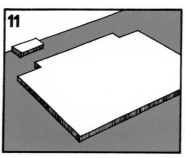

11

Plane plywood seat to exact size and cut away the corners illustrated with a back saw.

12

Glue 2 in. foam to plywood base, using a standard contact adhesive.

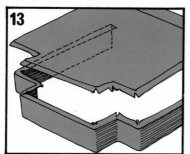

13

Cut out material for the cover, allowing $\frac{1}{2}$ in. for the fold back from the seam.

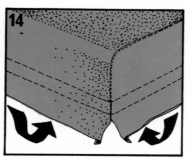

14

Machine sew the cover; position over foam. It should be a snug fit with the cover stretched uniformly over foam.

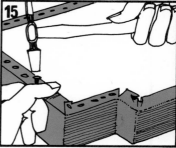

15

Turn the seat unit over and tack the cover to the underside of ply base, pulling it tight as you do so.

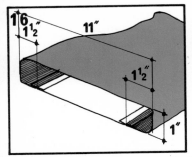

Machine sew together the sleeve for the back upholstery, using calico for the inside face as shown.

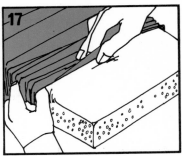

Pull the sleeve over the 1 in. thick foam back unit.

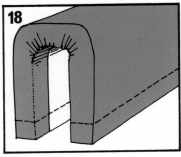

This will then be formed over the top back rail as shown.

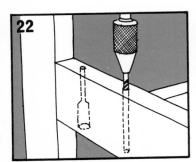

Round off the top corners with fine sand paper wrapped firmly around a cork sanding block.

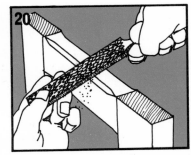

Take all the sharp corners off the top back rail with a rasp.

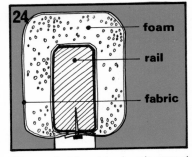

Sand down the whole job with medium fine sandpaper, taking off all sharp edges as you do so.

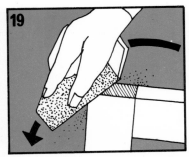

Drill out holes for screwing seat into position and deep countersink as illustrated.

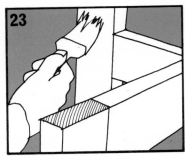

Coat the chair frame with 2 coats of polyurethane varnish, sanding down between each coat.

foam

rail

fabric

Wrap upholstered back unit around top back rail as shown in the above section.

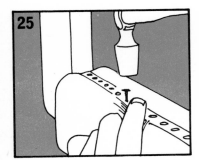

Fix in position by tacking through the cover to the underside of the rail. Use $\frac{3}{8}$ in. tacks.

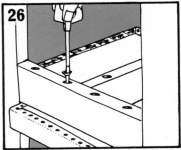

Turn chair upside down on to seat unit and screw into position using 2 in. woodscrews.

This chair is designed to match the table so it is finished in matte polyurethane varnish.

Dining Room Table

Three identical and free-standing doweled hardwood frames are used to support a glass table surface. The table, in two sections, can be used as illustrated to seat eight people. Without the smaller section linked to the larger, the table will seat six people. The small surface can then be used as a serving table.

MATERIALS (in inches)					TOOLS	OTHER REQUIREMENTS
no. off	l.	w.	th.	description		
6	33	$2\frac{1}{4}$	$1\frac{1}{4}$	framing	adjustable bevel	woodworking adhesive
9	28	$2\frac{1}{4}$	$1\frac{1}{4}$	framing	back saw	rubber feet (9)
6	17	$2\frac{1}{2}$	$1\frac{1}{4}$	framing	smoothing plane	rubber cushion pads (9)
3	48	$\frac{3}{8}$	dia.	dowel	brace	matte polyurethane varnish
1	48	36	$\frac{1}{2}$	plate glass	3/8 in. auger bit	2 in. brush
1	24	36	$\frac{1}{2}$	plate glass	sash cramps	pkg. panel pins
					trysquare.	
					miterblock	
					cork sanding block	

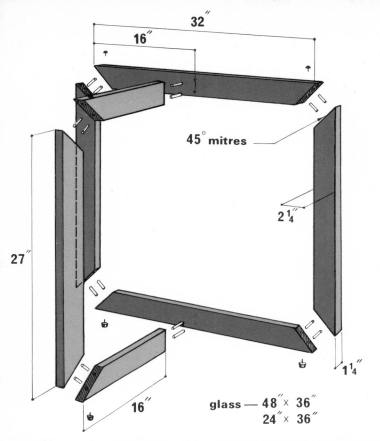

32″

16″

45° mitres

2 1/4″

27″

16″

1 1/4″

glass — 48″ × 36″
24″ × 36″

Mark out the lengths of wood and scribe the miter, using an adjustable bevel.

Cut the miters, using back saw and miter block.

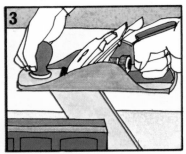

Plane the miters flat, using very sharp smoothing plane.

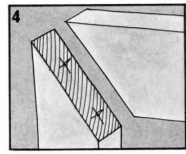

Mark out the positions of the dowels very carefully.

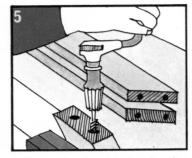

Drill out the dowel holes, keeping the drill at right angles to miter surface.

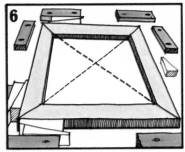

Using a cramping board (or alternatively sash cramps), glue the rectangular frames squarely together.

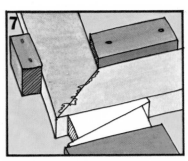

Detail of wedges used to apply pressure to the joint.

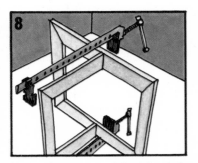

Use sash cramps to join right angle frame to the rectangular frame. Finish in matte polyurethane varnish.

Hat and Coat Stand

A simple tripod arrangement of three shaped boards glued and screwed to a hexagonal pole. Coats and purses are held on doweled pegs at the top of the unit. It can be painted in any color to enhance the decor of your room. The pegs can also be painted or coated with polyurethane lacquer.

MATERIALS (in inches)					TOOLS	OTHER REQUIREMENTS
no. off	l.	w.	th.	description		
3	72	$5\frac{1}{2}$	$\frac{3}{4}$	uprights	spokeshave	woodworking adhesive
3	17	$5\frac{1}{2}$	$\frac{3}{4}$	molded pieces	brace and $\frac{3}{4}$ in. auger bit	glasspaper
2	72	$1\frac{1}{2}$	$\frac{5}{8}$	spine	tenon saw	polyurethane paint
1	30	$\frac{3}{4}$	dia.	dowel	cork sanding block	$2\frac{1}{4}$ in. No. 10 countersunk
1	12	$2\frac{1}{2}$	dia.	dowel	coping saw	woodscrews (18)
					smoothing plane	

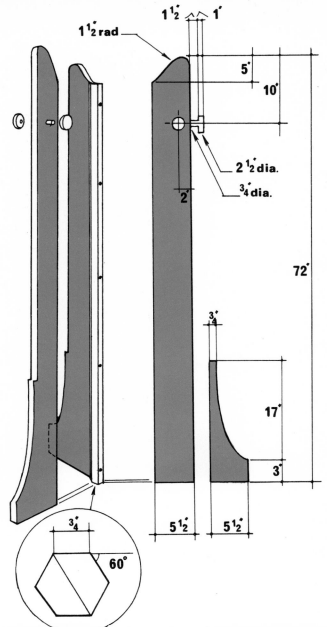

$1\frac{1}{2}$ rad

$1\frac{1}{2}''$ $1''$

$5''$

$10''$

$2\frac{1}{2}''$ dia.

$\frac{3}{4}''$ dia.

$2''$

$72''$

$\frac{3}{4}''$

$17''$

$3''$

$5\frac{1}{2}''$ $5\frac{1}{2}''$

$\frac{3}{4}''$

$60°$

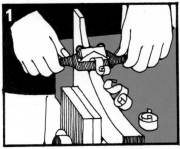

1

Mark out and cut flared base pieces. A spokeshave can be used to smooth the curved edges.

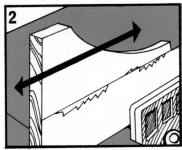

2

Glue flared pieces to the uprights by applying glue to both surfaces, 'rubbing' together in direction of arrows.

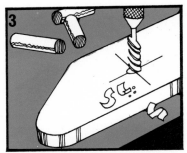

3

Mark out and drill holes for the coat pegs. Radius the top edges of uprights using a coping saw.

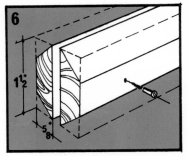

4

Cut the dowel caps and smooth the surface using fine sandpaper. Drill holes to take the dowels $\frac{1}{2}$ in. deep.

5

Assemble the stand by screwing through center post into edges of uprights. A painted finish is recommended.

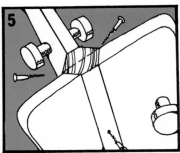

6

$1\frac{1}{2}$

$\frac{5}{8}$

A method of achieving the hexagonal post, by planing and then gluing together 2 strips, is shown here.

Chess Set

The chess set pieces can be made simply by using two wood-working processes — drilling and sawing. If fairly light colored hardwood is used, one half of the pieces can be left their natural color and the others stained black or red. The board is a piece of plywood with heavy lippings, and the squares are colored by using felt-tipped markers.

MATERIALS (in inches)					TOOLS	OTHER REQUIREMENTS
no. off	l.	w.	th.	description		
1	72	$1\frac{1}{4}$	$1\frac{1}{4}$	chessmen	try-square	woodworking adhesive
1	16	16	$\frac{1}{2}$	board	back saw	fine sand paper
4	20	$1\frac{3}{4}$	$\frac{3}{4}$	lippings	bench hook	black felt-tipped pen
					wheelbrace	cramping board and wedges
					$\frac{1}{4}$ in. drill bit	wood stain (red)
					cork sanding block	

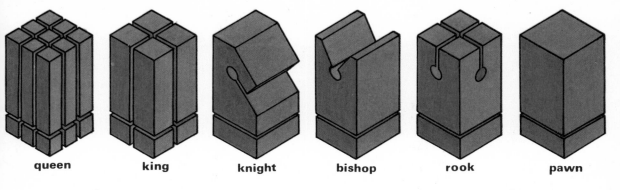

queen **king** **knight** **bishop** **rook** **pawn**

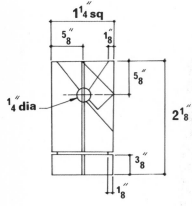

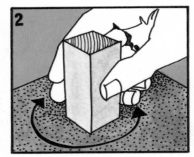

1
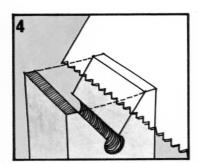
Square off the block pieces, using a trysquare

2
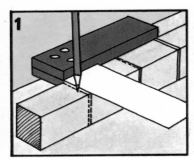
After cutting to size, using bench hook and back saw, sand down the end grain.

3

Place blocks in vise and saw or drill as the piece requires.

4
Square off the block pieces, using a trysquare
This view shows the making of a bishop piece. Sand down all pieces, stain half the set.

5

Mark out the board into 2 in. squares and mark alternate ones with felt pen.

6

A homemade cramping board using wedges will serve to cramp the lippings when being glued.

Steps

The household steps made from softwood are suitable for various domestic jobs, from home decorating and maintenance to climbing into attics. They can be used safely as trestles in conjunction with scaffold boards for ceiling work. The steps consist of two identical halves and so are easily and quickly constructed.

MATERIALS (in inches)					TOOLS	OTHER REQUIREMENTS
no. off	l.	w.	th.	description		
4	48	$4\frac{3}{4}$	$\frac{3}{4}$	sides	try-square	woodworking adhesive
10	16	6	$\frac{3}{4}$	steps	adjustable bevel	2 in. No. 10 brass countersunk
					smoothing plane	screws (40)
					back saw	$\frac{3}{8}$ in. No. 8 brass countersunk
					$\frac{1}{2}$ in. beveled edge chisel	screws (12)
					cork sanding block	One pair 8 in. trestle hinges
					bench hook	fine sand paper
					screwdriver	polyurethane clear matte varnish
						brass cup washers (40)

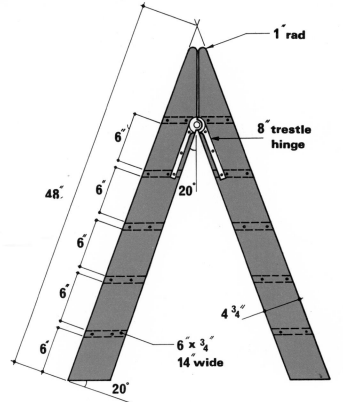

1″ rad

8″ trestle hinge

48″

6″

6″

6″

6″

6″

6″

20°

20°

4 $\frac{3}{4}$″

6″ x $\frac{3}{4}$″

14″ wide

1

Mark out uprights using an adjustable bevel set at 20°.

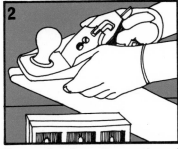

2

Cut to size then plane and sand edges.

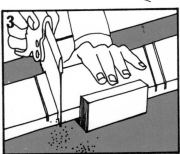

3

Cut sides of housings using a back saw.

4

Chisel out housings, using beveled-edge chisel.

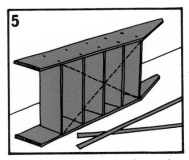

5

Screw two halves together using 2 in. No. 10 brass screws and cup washers, and check for squareness, using 'diagonal test.'

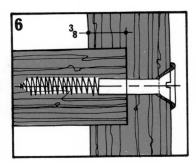

6

$\frac{3}{8}$

View showing screw with brass cup washer, holding step treads to uprights.

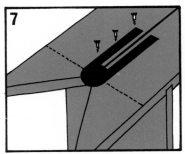

7

Fit trestle hinges, using $\frac{3}{4}$ in. No. 8 brass screws, their centers on corners of the uprights.

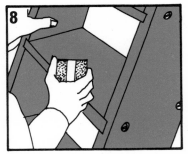

8

Sand down with fine sandpaper and cork block, then coat with polyurethane varnish.

Screen with a View

Panels of soft-board glued back-to-back provide lightweight but rigid elements for the domestic screen. A group of five panels can be painted with the design shown, or with one of your own choice. The screen can be used in a variety of ways where temporary partitioning is required in the home.

MATERIALS (in inches)					TOOLS	OTHER REQUIREMENTS
no. off	l.	w.	th.	description		
10	72	18	$\frac{3}{8}$	soft-board	smoothing plane cork sanding block craft knife small G-cramp	1 in. canvas webbing (12 yds) fine sandpaper woodworking adhesive clear sealer contact adhesive 3 in. paint brush aerosol paint cans cardboard for surface design
10	$1\frac{1}{4}$	$\frac{3}{4}$	$\frac{3}{8}$	feet		

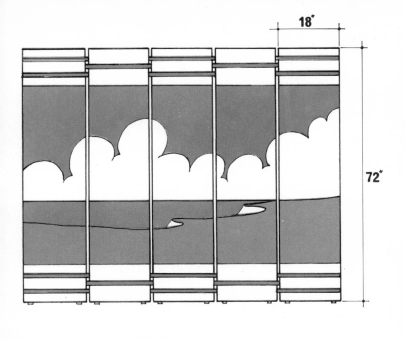

18"

72"

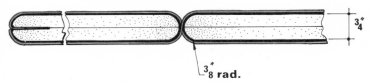

$\frac{3}{4}$"

$\frac{3}{8}$" **rad.**

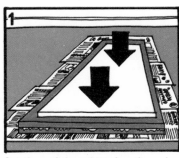

1

Cut the soft-board to size, then glue together, using contact adhesive, with finished surfaces outwards.

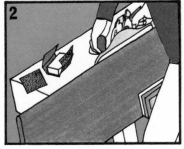

2

Round off the long edges, using fine sandpaper or a sharp smoothing plane.

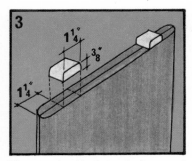

3

$1\frac{1}{4}$" $\frac{3}{8}$"

$1\frac{1}{4}$"

Glue wooden blocks to the base and sand down when set.

4

Seal surfaces of the panels with a clear sealer. When dry, sand down using fine sandpaper.

5

Cut surface design in cardboard and place on board. Apply colors, using aerosol paint. Repeat on reverse surfaces.

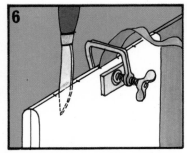

6

Using a knife, pry open panels and tuck in webbing in the required position on the end 2 boards and glue.

7

'Weave' 1 in. canvas webbing through the panels and glue to surface.

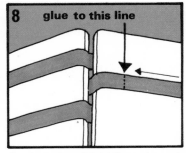

8

glue to this line

To aid successful folding, glue only up to the line shown.

Stackable Stool

These stools can be used in the kitchen/breakfast room situation as dining seats. The seating height is such that they relate to a normal 28 to 30 in. high table. In making them up, ensure that the angle between leg and under-rail is 90° exactly — if it is less than a right angle, the stackability will be impaired.

MATERIALS (in inches)					TOOLS	OTHER REQUIREMENTS
no. off	l.	w.	th.	description		

3	17	2¾	¾	legs (deal)	try-square
					plane
					back saw
					coping saw
					marking gauge
					⅜ in. beveled edge chisel
					wheelbrace and bits
					screwdriver
					sewing machine
					G-cramp
					cork sanding block
					countersink
						contact adhesive
						woodworking adhesive
						matte polyurethane varnish
						1 in. paint brush
						1½ in. No. 10 countersunk
						  woodscrews (12)
						2 in. No. 10 countersunk
						  woodscrews (6)
						fine sandpaper
						9 in. strip of 'Velcro' tape
						wood filler
						needle and thread

3	9	2¾	¾	rails (deal)		
3	4	1¼	1¼	triangular blocks		
1	12	12	¾	seat plywood		
1	13	dia.	2	foam med. density		
1	30	15	—	fabric		

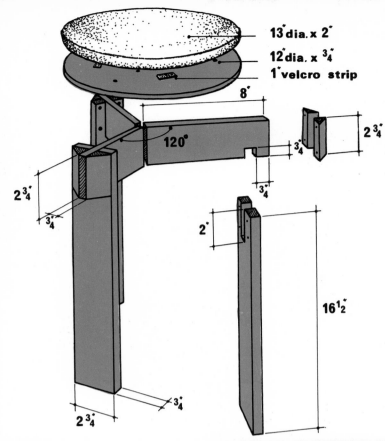

13˝dia. x 2˝
12˝dia. x ³⁄₄˝
1˝ velcro strip

8˝

120°

2³⁄₄˝

³⁄₄˝

3˝

3˝

2³⁄₄˝

2˝

16¹⁄₂˝

³⁄₄˝

2³⁄₄˝

³⁄₄˝

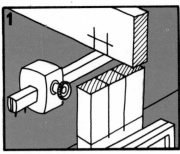

1 Mark out halving joints between legs and seat rails, using marking gauge and trysquare.

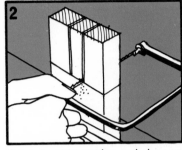

2 Cut out center section and clean up base and side of cut-out with chisel.

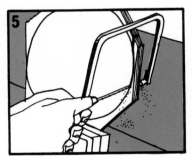

5 Mark out and cut circular seat using a fret or coping saw.

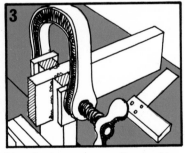

3 Glue the legs to seat rails, checking for squareness before cramping.

4 Glue and screw the triangular fillets into position. Use 1¹⁄₂ in. woodscrews.

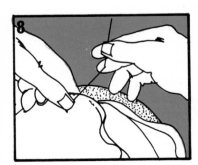

6 Glue and screw the seat to the legs using 2 in. No. 10 woodscrews.

7 Cut out fairly dense circle of foam and apply adhesive to edge. When sticky, pinch surfaces together.

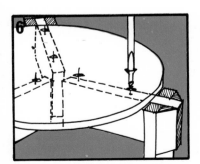

8 Stitch cover together leaving an opening for the foam. Place foam into cushion and slip-stitch the opening.

Kitchen Cupboard

The cabinet is designed for storing food packages, cans and bottles. It is of strong construction in plywood and softwood and can be very easily assembled. The finished unit is wall mounted for maximum space saving.

no. off	MATERIALS (in inches)				TOOLS	OTHER REQUIREMENTS
	l.	w.	th.	description		

2	55	15	$\frac{1}{2}$	plytop and bottom	try-square
					back saw
					bench hook
					hammer
					punch
					$\frac{3}{8}$ in. beveled edge chisel
					rip saw
					masonry drill bit
					wheelbrace and drill bits
					smoothing plane
					screwdriver
					compass
					pad saw
						woodworking adhesive
						2 in. brass butt hinges (12)
						masking tape
						aerosol paint cans
						pkg. panel pins
						fine sandpaper
						magnetic catches (6)
						rawl plugs
						$\frac{3}{8}$ in. No. 8 brass countersunk
						   woodscrews (72)
						$1\frac{1}{2}$ in. No. 10 steel countersunk
						   woodscrews (36)
						$2\frac{1}{2}$ in. No. 10 steel countersunk
						   woodscrews (6)

8	24	15	$\frac{1}{8}$	ply panels		
6	26	8	$\frac{1}{2}$	ply doors		
1	55	24	$\frac{1}{8}$	ply back		
2	12	15	$\frac{1}{2}$	ply shelves		
8	24	$1\frac{1}{4}$	$1\frac{1}{4}$	deal timbers		
8	15	$1\frac{1}{4}$	$1\frac{1}{4}$	deal timbers		
4	25	$1\frac{1}{2}$	$\frac{1}{2}$	deal lippings		
3	55	$2\frac{3}{4}$	$\frac{3}{4}$	deal backrails		
1	48	$\frac{1}{4}$	$\frac{1}{4}$	deal shelf supports		

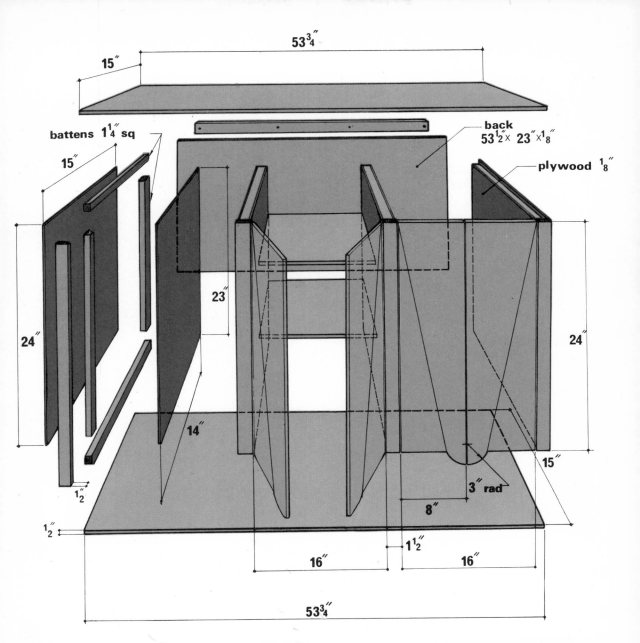

53 3/4"

15"

back
53 1/2" × 23" × 1/8"

battens 1 1/4" sq

15"

plywood 1/8"

24"

23"

24"

14"

1/2"

3" rad

15"

1/2"

8"

1 1/2"

16"

16"

53 3/4"

1 Cut vertical panel boards to size using rip saw. Check for squareness using trysquare.

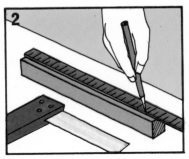

2 Mark out the pieces of timber for vertical panels.

3 Cut timbers to length using back saw and a bench hook.

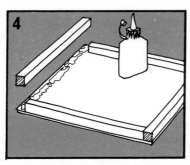

4 Fabricate vertical panels. Leave the outside ply sheets off the 2 end panels.

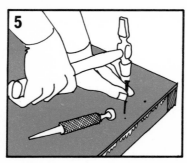

5 Glue and pin the vertical panels. Then punch the panel pins just below the surface.

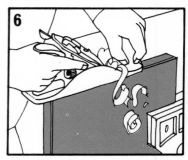

6 Plane up the edges, using a smoothing plane.

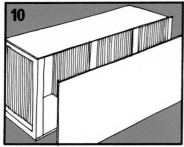

7 Mark out the top and base boards.

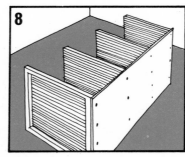

8 Screw and glue base to vertical panels. Use $1\frac{1}{2}$ in. woodscrews.

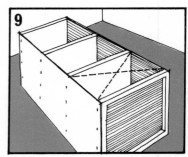

9 Glue and screw top into position and check for squareness. Use $1\frac{1}{2}$ in. woodscrews.

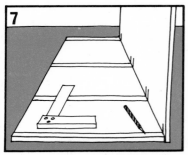

10 Rip saw the back to size, trim with smoothing plane and screw into position. Use $\frac{3}{4}$ in. woodscrews.

11 Screw and glue the top timber to the back; use $\frac{3}{4}$ in. woodscrews. Note the slope planed on the lower edge.

12 Screw and glue bottom timber to the back; use $\frac{3}{4}$ in. woodscrews.

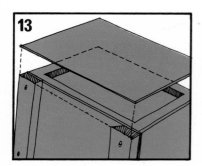

13 Trim the end sheets to size, glue and pin into position.

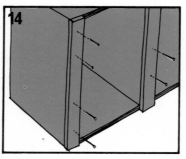

14 Glue and pin the vertical pieces between the doors into position.

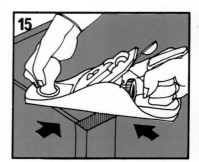

15 Plane the end grain flush with the top and base, taking care not to split the wood.

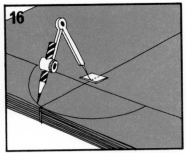

16 Mark out the doors slightly oversize. Use compass for scribing semi-circular detail.

17 Place the doors in the vise and cut out the handle profiles. Use pad saw for curves.

pad saw

tenon saw

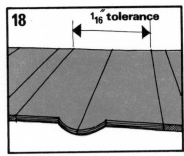

18 $\frac{1}{16}''$ tolerance

Place the cabinet on its side and plane down door edges until a good fit is achieved.

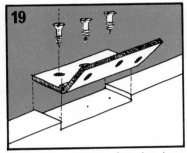

19 Make the cut-outs for the butt hinges in the doors using a saw and chisel. Loosely screw hinges on.

20 Place doors into position on cabinet and mark position of hinge cut-outs on the vertical pieces between the doors.

21 Make cut-outs and loosely screw hinges. Check action of the doors. Once satisfactory, remove doors for painting.

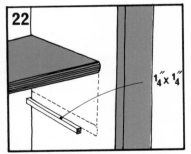

22 $\frac{1}{4}'' \times \frac{1}{4}''$

Thin timbers, glued and tacked into position, hold the shelves.

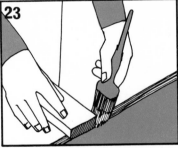

23 Sand down and paint the cabinet inside and out.

24 Sand down, mask and spray-paint the doors.

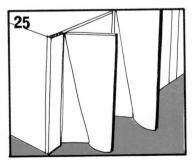

25 Fit the doors. Magnetic catches can be fitted to hold them shut.

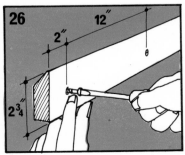

26 12"   2"   2$\frac{3}{4}''$

Mark position of cabinet on the wall. Drill and plug holes. Screw wall timber into position. Use 2$\frac{1}{2}$ in. No. 10 woodscrews.

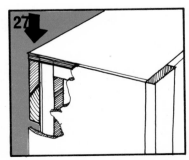

27 Lift cabinet into position and check that it hangs safely.

Spice Rack

The containers are simply designed to hold herbs and spices and fit into a rack varying in length according to the number of varieties stored. The rack can be screwed to the wall above a work surface allowing easy access. The use of a cork to locate the lid also serves to keep the contents fresh.

MATERIALS (in inches)					TOOLS	OTHER REQUIREMENTS
no. off	l.	w.	th.	description		
1	24	$2\frac{1}{4}$	$2\frac{1}{4}$	jars	back saw	woodworking adhesives
1	12	$4\frac{1}{4}$	$\frac{3}{8}$	rack back	smoothing plane	pkg. panel pins
1	12	$2\frac{3}{4}$	$\frac{3}{8}$	rack bottom	brace and forstner bit	1 in. No. 6 countersunk
1	12	$\frac{3}{4}$	$\frac{3}{8}$	rack lip	screwdriver	woodscrews (12)
5	$1\frac{3}{4}$	dia.	—	corks	cork sanding block	fine sandpaper
5	$1\frac{3}{4}$	$1\frac{3}{4}$	$\frac{1}{8}$	plywood bottoms	trysquare	contact adhesive
					bench hook	rawl plugs (2)
					wheelbrace and drill bits	adhesive name lables
					countersink	$1\frac{1}{2}$ in. No. 8 countersunk
					masonry drill bit	woodscrews (2)

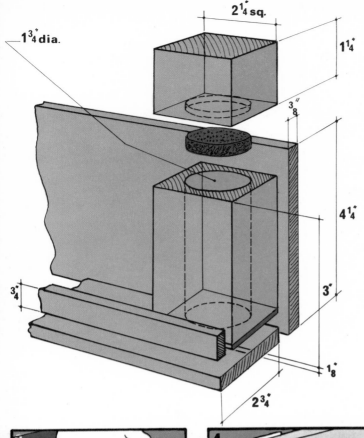

2¼" sq.

1¾" dia.

1¼"

3⅜"

4¼"

3"

¾"

⅛"

2¾"

Mark out timber with a trysquare and cut to lengths shown in the diagram, leaving a tolerance for planing down.

Plane down square sections to marked lines. Work against scrap wood to avoid splitting the end grain.

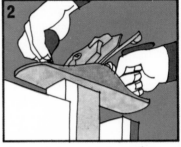

Screw and glue the front lipping to the base and, when dry, sand down using a fine grade sandpaper.

Mark the center of the blocks, then place in vise. Using a brace and forstner bit, drill the holes.

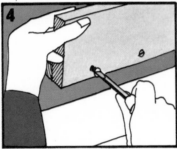

Cut wood for rack to length required (in multiples of 2¼ in.). Screw and glue base of rack to the back.

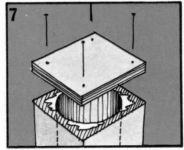

Screw and glue the front lipping to the base and, when dry, sand down using a fine grade sandpaper.

Drill ¼ in. recess into lid. Fix cork in recess with contact adhesive.

Glue and pin the hardboard square to the base of container and sand down flush.

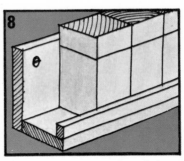

Sand down all wood and leave untreated. Fix self-adhesive labels to containers. Drill and plug wall; screw rack to it.

Food Preparation Table

This table, covered with ceramic tiles, can be used equally well in traditional or modern 'built-in' kitchens. The surface wipes clean easily and will not stain, making the table ideal for preparing meat, vegetables, etc. The unit is constructed of blockboard held together by blocks, glued and screwed in the corners.

MATERIALS (in inches)					TOOLS	OTHER REQUIREMENTS
no. off	l.	w.	th.	description		
1	26	26	$\frac{1}{2}$	ply top	back saw	woodworking adhesive
2	32	17	$\frac{1}{2}$	ply sides	bench hook	ceramic tiles (200)
2	32	$15\frac{1}{2}$	$\frac{1}{2}$	ply sides	screwdriver	cement adhesive
4	26	8	$\frac{1}{2}$	ply top sides	smoothing plane	tile grouting
4	32	$\frac{3}{4}$	$\frac{3}{4}$	deal timbers	wheelbrace	1 in. No. 8 countersunk
5	24	$\frac{3}{4}$	$\frac{3}{4}$	deal timbers	countersink	woodscrews (80)
2	16	$\frac{3}{4}$	$\frac{3}{4}$	deal battens	$\frac{3}{16}$ in. drill bit	

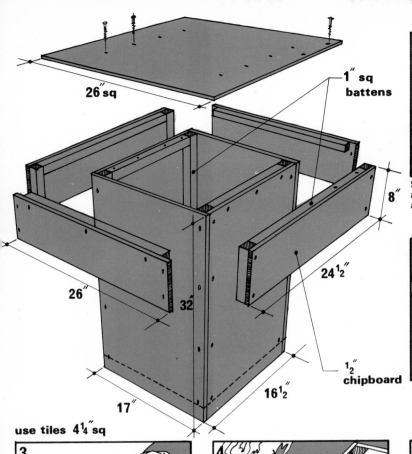

26" sq

1" sq battens

8"

26"

32"

24½"

½" chipboard

17"

16½"

use tiles 4¼" sq

1 Square off the ends of all timbers and cut to length, using bench hook and back saw.

2 Glue and screw timbers to top sides, using 1 in. No. 8 steel woodscrews.

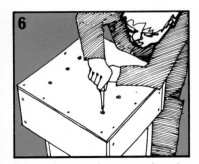

3 Clean down with a smoothing plane. Work from both ends so the wood does not split at ends.

4 Glue and screw timbers to 16½ in. width panels and assemble main box support.

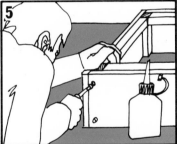

5 Construct the top by gluing and screwing pieces together. Plane edges flush.

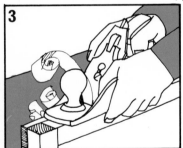

6 Glue and screw the two main units together. Countersink all screw-heads below the surface.

7 Lay ceramic tiles, using the recommended adhesive. Tiles begin 2 in. from ground level.

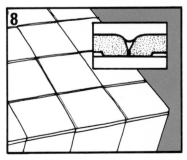

8 Grout all tile joints, rubbing well into each joint with a damp cloth.

Clothes Rack

One of the simpler projects in the book, the clothes rack consists of three identical frames hinged to one another with brightly colored webbing. It provides a hanging rack for clothes before and after ironing. It can be arranged to stand in a triangular or zig-zag plan, and when not in use packs flat for storage.

MATERIALS (in inches)					TOOLS	OTHER REQUIREMENTS
no. off	l.	w.	th.	description		
6	60	1½	1½	deal uprights	marking knife back saw bench hook ¾ in. beveled edge chisel brace ½ in. auger bit hammer mallet	woodworking adhesive ½ in. tacks fine sandpaper polyurethane varnish
15	20	½	dia.	dowel		
1	56	6	—	canvas webbing		

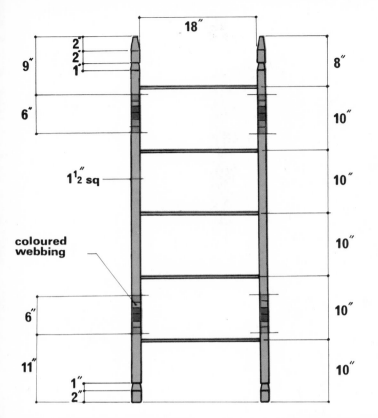

18″

9″ 2″ 2″ 1″

8″

6″

10″

1 1/2″ sq

10″

coloured webbing

10″

6″

10″

11″

10″

1″ 2″

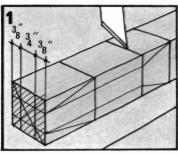

1 3/8″ 3/4″ 3/8″

Cut uprights to length and mark out the decorative detail.

2

Hold wood in bench hook and, using a back saw, make the horizontal cuts.

3

Chisel the chamfers, using a beveled edge chisel.

4

Drill the holes for the horizontal rails in the uprights, to depth of 1 in.

5

Make up a cramping board and assemble the 3 frames. Check for squareness.

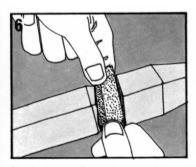

6

Sand down all surfaces and coat with polyurethane varnish.

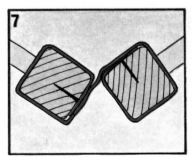

7

Join the 3 frames together, using webbing tacked as shown above.

8

(Colored webbing is shown above being tacked into position.)

Pocket Wall Board

Leather pouches of various sizes laced to a shaped plywood board provide handy pockets for many bits and pieces found in a kitchen. The cork panel provides a pin-up space for shopping lists, messages and reminders, and the row of hooks at the base can hold mugs or larger utensils.

MATERIALS (in inches)					TOOLS	OTHER REQUIREMENTS
no. off	l.	w.	th.	description		
1	34	24	$\frac{3}{8}$	base board	back saw	woodworking adhesive
1	26	$2\frac{1}{2}$	$\frac{3}{4}$	timber	pad saw	$1\frac{1}{2}$ in. No. 10 brass countersunk
1	30	12	$\frac{1}{2}$	pin board	spokeshave	woodscrews (6)
1	60	5	$\frac{1}{16}+$	leather pockets	wheelbrace	brass cup washers (2)
					$\frac{1}{16}$ in. drill bit	brass hooks (7)
					countersink	Yards $\frac{1}{8}$ in. dia. cord (7 yds)
					screwdriver	fine sandpaper
					knife	polyurethane varnish or paint
					bradawl	rawl plugs (2)
					needles	
					cork, sanding block	
					masonry drill bit	

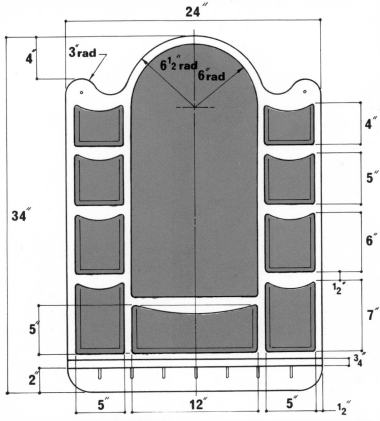

24"

4"

3" rad

6 1/2" rad

6" rad

34"

4"

5"

6"

1/2"

7"

3/4"

5"

2"

5"

12"

5"

1/2"

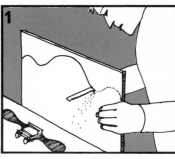

1

Mark out ply board and cut out profile. Smooth with spokeshave and fine sandpaper. Paint or varnish.

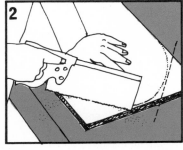

2

Mark out and cut cork to correct size.

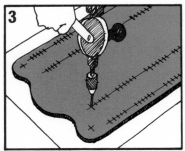

3

Mark out positions of pouches and drill holes for thread at $\frac{1}{2}$ in. intervals; use $\frac{1}{16}$ in. drill.

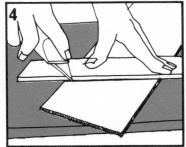

4

Cut out leather pouches. Slope sides so that they bulge out when fixed.

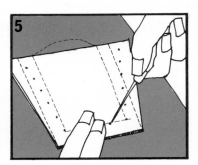

5

Pierce leather with bradawl around edges.

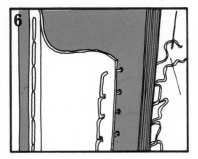

6

Using a heavy thread, sew on the leather pouches.

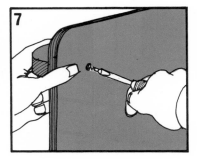

7

Cut and round off edges on the small shelf. Screw on hooks and fix shelf to board. Screw from behind using 4 screws.

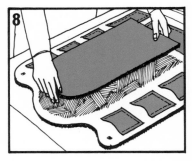

8

Glue cork pin-board into position. Fix board to wall.

Child's Desk

Two small pieces of plywood cut out in the manner shown opposite provide all the component parts for the child's desk. The finished article may be stained, painted, or coated with a clear polyurethane lacquer. The size of the desk makes it suitable for use by children between the ages of *five and seven*.

MATERIALS (in inches)					TOOLS	OTHER REQUIREMENTS
no. off	l.	w.	th.	description		
2	25	21	$\frac{3}{4}$	panels	trysquare brace and straight-sided bit $\frac{1}{2}$ in. beveled edge chisel screwdriver cork sanding block wheelbrace and drill bits smoothing plane pad saw or electric jig saw	woodworking adhesive $1\frac{1}{2}$ in. No. 6 countersunk woodscrews (18) standard wood filler polyurethane paint or varnish 2 in. brush fine sandpaper **plastic wood filler**

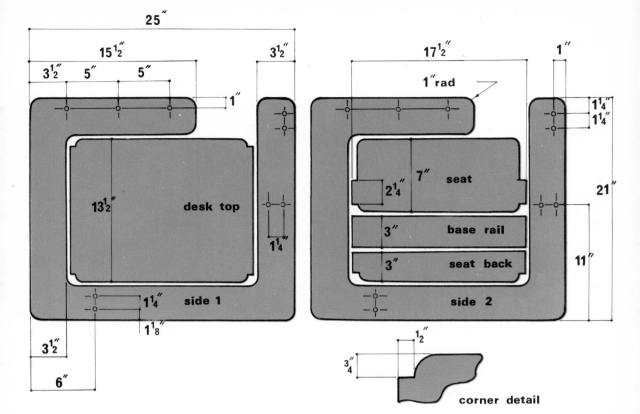

25″

15½″ 3½″

3½″ 5″ 5″

1″

desk top

13½″

1″

1¼″

side 1

1¼″

1⅛″

3½″

6″

17½″ 1″

1″ rad

1¼″
1¼″

2¼″ 7″ seat

base rail

3″

3″ seat back

21″

11″

side 2

½″

¾″

corner detail

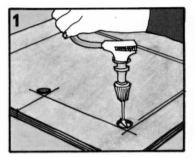

1

Mark out the 2 boards as shown above. Drill corners with ½ in. (12 mm) straight-sided bit in a brace.

2

Cut out profiles, using a pad saw or an electric jig-saw.

3

Chisel out the corner details, plane and sand down the edges.

4

Drill and countersink the holes in the 2 side pieces. Use ⅛ in. (3 mm) drill.

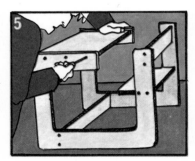

5

Screw the structure together, using No. 6 woodscrews 1½ in. (38 mm) long. Fill the holes with matching woodfiller.

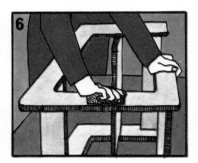

6

Sand down all surfaces and edges. Coat with polyurethane varnish or paint.

Hall Mirror

This particular mirror is for use in a hall or lobby. Its simple halving joint construction means it can be made by someone with minimum wood-working knowledge. The spaces between the frames can be used to store small objects, clothes brushes, etc. The whole frame is made from standard deal.

MATERIALS (in inches)					TOOLS	OTHER REQUIREMENTS
no. off	l.	w.	th.	description		
4	30	$1\frac{3}{4}$	$\frac{3}{8}$	vertical framing	try-square back saw screwdriver	woodworking adhesive $1\frac{1}{4}$ in. No. 6 countersunk woodscrews (8)
4	20	$1\frac{3}{4}$	$\frac{3}{8}$	horizontal framing	wheelbrace bench hook	fine sandpaper polyurethane paint or varnish
3	24	$\frac{1}{2}$	$\frac{1}{4}$	beading	marking gauge	1 in. paint brush
1	12	2	$\frac{3}{4}$	corner blocks	cork sanding block $\frac{1}{8}$ in. drill bit	
1	20	10	—	mirror	countersink $\frac{1}{4}$ in. beveled edge chisel	

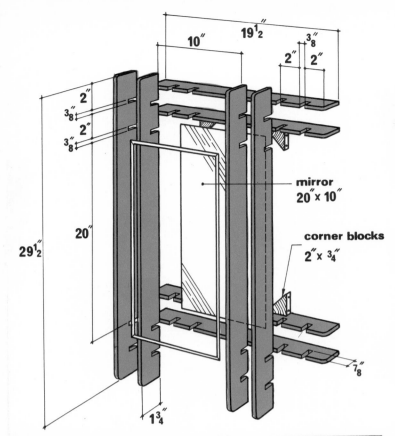

mirror
20″ x 10″

corner blocks
2″ x 3/4″

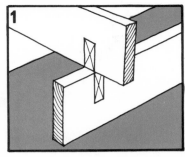

1

Cut pieces of wood to length and mark out halving joints, using try-square, pencil and marking gauge.

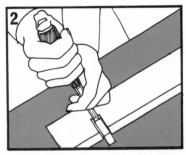

2

Saw and chisel out the halving joints.

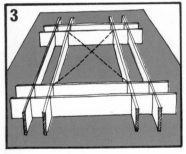

3

Glue the pieces together, cleaning off surplus glue. Check for squareness, using the 'diagonal test.'

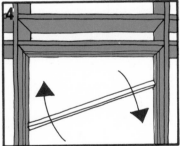

4

Cut to size and glue in the beading to hold the mirror.

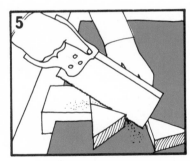

5

Mark out and cut the 4 corner blocks.

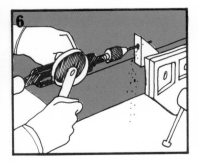

6

Drill the corner blocks to take No. 6 woodscrews and countersink the holes.

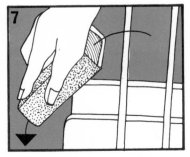

7

Sand down the mirror frame and paint, or coat with clear polyurethane varnish.

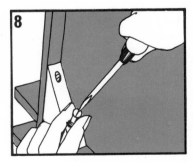

8

Fit mirror and screw in the corner blocks to hold it in place. Use No. 6 woodscrews.

Baby Sleeper

The baby sleeper is a simple crib for use by children up to the age of about two and a half. The conventional bars are replaced by washable canvas panels, screwed to the inside frames. The front one has a clear vinyl observation window sewn into it. The frames are of standard deal, the base and end panels made from plywood.

MATERIALS (in inches)					TOOLS	OTHER REQUIREMENTS
no. off	l.	w.	th.	description		
4	33	$5\frac{3}{4}$	$\frac{3}{4}$	legs	mortise gauge	woodworking adhesive
2	40	$4\frac{3}{4}$	$\frac{3}{4}$	side rails	$\frac{1}{4}$ in. mortise chisel	$1\frac{1}{2}$ in. No. 8 countersunk
2	$22\frac{1}{2}$	$22\frac{1}{2}$	$\frac{1}{2}$	end panels	back saw compass	woodscrews (20) $\frac{3}{4}$ in. No. 8 brass countersunk
1	40	$22\frac{1}{2}$	$\frac{1}{2}$	mattress support	rasp $\frac{1}{2}$ in. beveled edge chisel	woodscrews (16) small brass eyelets (16)
3	46	$\frac{3}{4}$	$\frac{3}{4}$	timbers	brace and straight-sided bit	$\frac{1}{2}$ in. tacks
1	80	40	—	canvas	screwdriver sewing machine	standard wood filler fine sandpaper
2	38	1	$\frac{1}{4}$	laths	cork sanding block	aerosol paint cans (lead free)
1	30	20	—	clear vinyl	bench hook	
1	40	$22\frac{1}{2}$	3	foam mattress	wheelbrace and drill bits panel saw	
1	108	36	—	fabric for mattress	pad saw countersink	

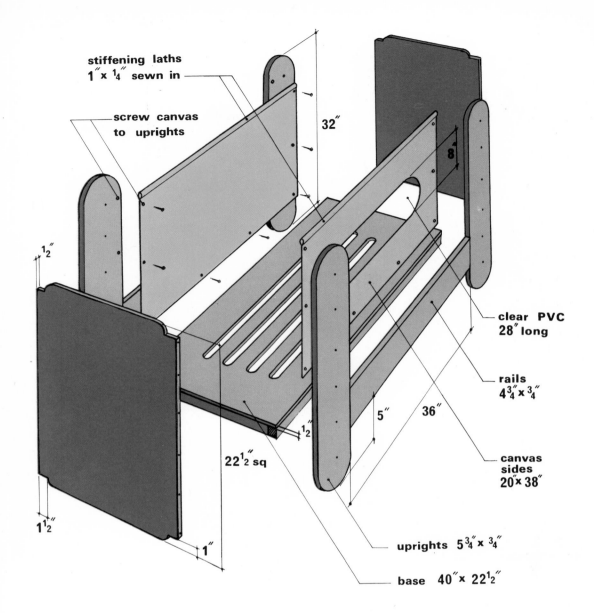

stiffening laths
1″ x 1/4″ sewn in

screw canvas
to uprights

32″

8″

clear PVC
28″ long

rails
4 3/4″ x 3/4″

canvas
sides
20″ x 38″

uprights 5 3/4″ x 3/4″

base 40″ x 22 1/2″

1/2″

1 1/2″

1″

22 1/2″ sq

5″

36″

1/2″

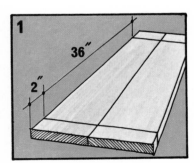

Mark out and cut legs and rails to size. Allow 1 1/2 in. at the end of each rail for the tenon.

36″

2″

Set a mortise gauge to a 1/4 in. mortise chisel.

Gauge mortise and tenon positions on all legs and rails.

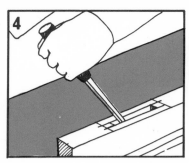

4

Cramp crib leg firmly in the vise and chop out mortise to a depth of 1 in.

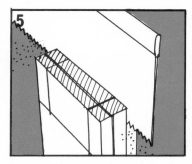

5

Cramp rail in vise and cut tenon. Cut down the grain first and then, using a bench hook, cut shoulders of joint.

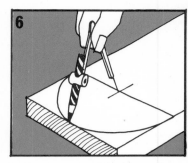

6

Radius the ends of the legs, using a compass.

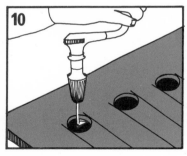

7

Cut away waste wood with a back saw and round off to the line with a rasp.

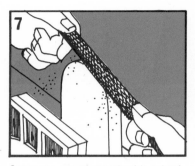

8

Cramp up the front and back frames using blocks and wedges or sash cramps. Check for squareness.

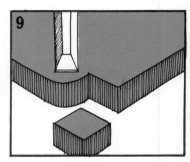

9

Shape plywood end panels by cutting out with a back saw and then paring down with a beveled edge chisel.

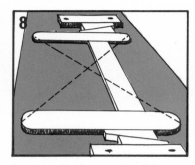

10

Mark out cut-outs on plywood base and drill holes at each end, using a brace and straight-sided bit.

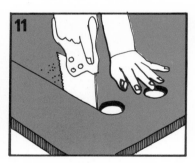

11

Cut out slots, beginning with a pad saw and finishing with a panel saw. Sand down all edges.

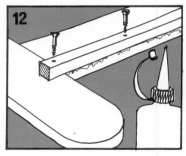

12

Screw and glue $\frac{7}{8}$ in. square timbers into position on both front and back frames and end panels.

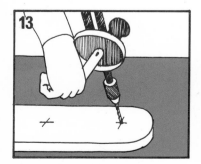

13

Drill and countersink screw hole positions for screwing end panels to leg frames.

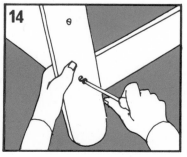

14

Glue and screw leg frames to end panels, using $1\frac{1}{2}$ in. No. 8 steel countersunk screws.

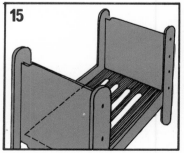

15

Glue and tack plywood base to timbers.

16

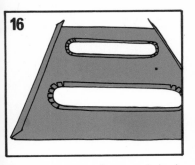

Cut out canvas front and back, allowing for a $1\frac{1}{4}$ in. seam down each side and a $\frac{5}{8}$ in. seam around the window.

17

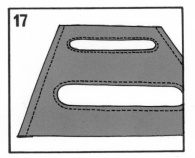

Machine sew seams down 1 in. from the edge on the length and $\frac{3}{8}$ in. on the cut-out.

18

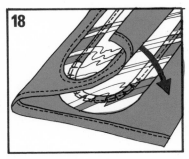

Cut out vinyl window and place in position. Fold over the canvas cut-out so that the 2 are in alignment.

19

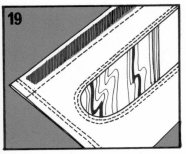

Stitch in window and stiffening lathe along top edge. Seam each side to complete the panel.

20

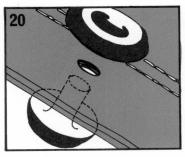

Fit $\frac{1}{2}$ in. diameter brass eyelets to edge of the panel.

21

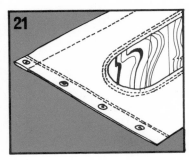

These should be placed at 6 in. intervals, starting from the top.

22

Fill all screw holes with wood filler and sand down the whole crib. Round off all sharp edges.

23

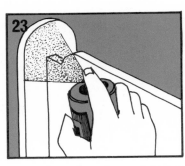

Spray the crib, using a lead-free paint of your own choice.

24

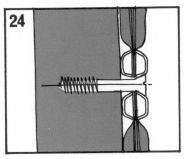

Screw in canvas panels using $\frac{3}{4}$ in. brass woodscrews.

25

Put in the top screw each side first and work downwards, pulling the panel tight as you go.

26

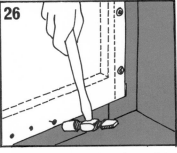

Tack along the bottom edge at 2 in. intervals, using $\frac{1}{2}$ in. tacks.

27

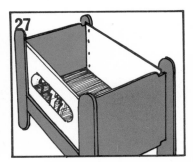

Use fabric to make mattress cover. Fit over foam and place in baby sleeper.

Child's Storage Trays

Four brightly painted boxes which stack on top of one another provide storage space for children's toys and play-things. The casters fitted to the largest box make the unit mobile even when fully loaded.

no. off	l.	w.	th.	description	TOOLS	OTHER REQUIREMENTS
6	33	$5\frac{1}{4}$	$\frac{3}{4}$	fronts and backs (deal)	back saw	cardboard for template
2	33	$11\frac{1}{4}$	$\frac{3}{4}$	fronts and back (ply)	bench hook	$2\frac{1}{2}$ in. casters (4)
6	20	$5\frac{3}{8}$	$\frac{3}{4}$	sides (deal)	coping saw	aerosol paint cans (lead free)
2	20	$11\frac{1}{4}$	$\frac{3}{4}$	sides (ply)	trysquare	standard wood filler
4	18	21	$\frac{1}{4}$	bottoms (ply)	marking gauge	woodworking adhesive
1	18	16	$\frac{1}{4}$	top lid (ply)	hammer	$1\frac{1}{2}$ in. panel pins ($\frac{1}{2}$ lb.)
3	78	$\frac{3}{4}$	$\frac{3}{4}$	timbers (deal)	punch	$1\frac{1}{2}$ in. No. 8 countersunk
1	78	$1\frac{7}{8}$	$1\frac{7}{8}$	timber	smoothing plane	woodscrews (12)
					screwdriver	fine sandpaper
					$\frac{3}{4}$ in. beveled edge chisel	
					cork sanding block	

MATERIALS (in inches)

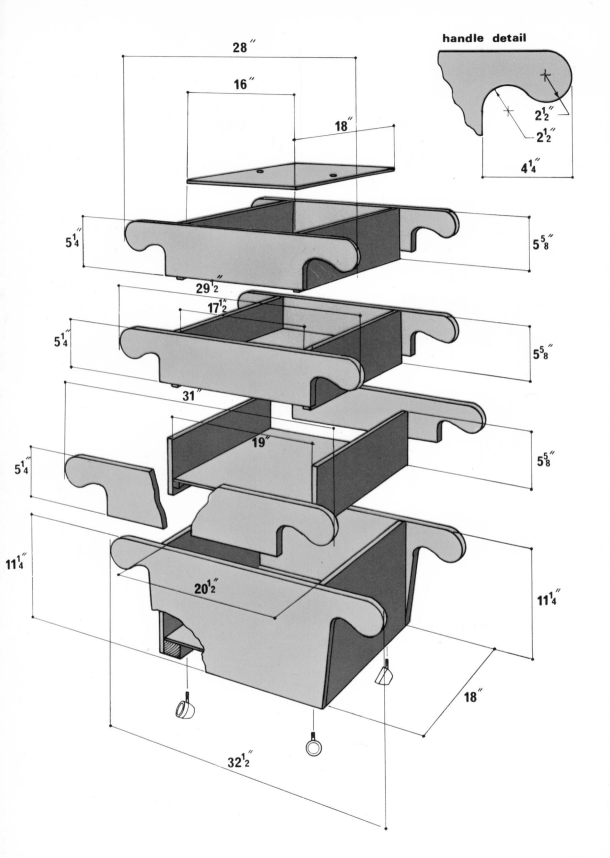

handle detail

$2\frac{1}{2}''$

$2\frac{1}{2}''$

$4\frac{1}{4}''$

$28''$

$16''$

$18''$

$5\frac{1}{4}''$

$5\frac{5}{8}''$

$29\frac{1}{2}''$

$17\frac{1}{2}''$

$5\frac{1}{4}''$

$5\frac{5}{8}''$

$31''$

$19''$

$5\frac{1}{4}''$

$5\frac{5}{8}''$

$11\frac{1}{4}''$

$20\frac{1}{2}''$

$11\frac{1}{4}''$

$18''$

$32\frac{1}{2}''$

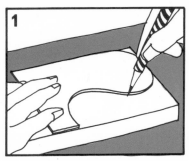

1

Cut out handle template in cardboard. Use it to mark out handles.

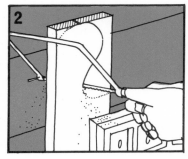

2

Saw down the handle cut-out.

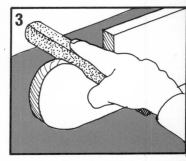

3

Sand down the handle cut-out, using fine sandpaper.

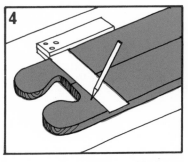

4

Place box sides together. Mark out position of box ends with trysquare..

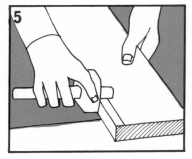

5

Scribe line marking position of timber holding base.

6

Glue and pin timbers to end pieces.

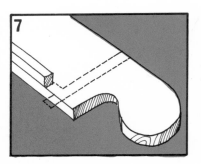

7

Glue and tack timbers to side pieces. Note where timbers end.

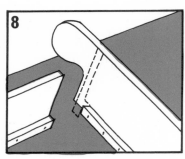

8

Check that sides and ends of boxes fit together.

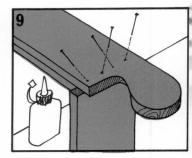

9

Glue and 'dovetail nail' sides and ends together using panel pins.

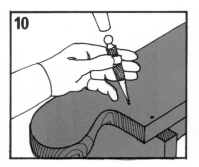

10

Push panel pin heads below the surface, using a nail-punch.

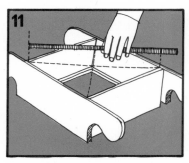

11

Before glue sets, check for squareness, using the 'diagonal test.' Rectify if not square.

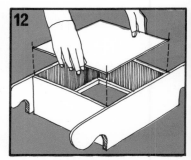

12

Cut ply bases to size and place into boxes.

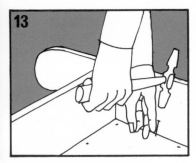

13

Tack down ply base to timbers using panel pins.

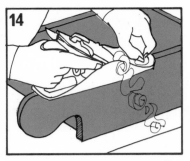

14

Clean up box, using smoothing plane and fine sandpaper.

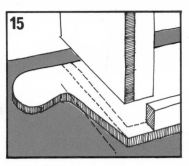

15

Repeat previous procedure for large box at the base. Note sloping of edge on box sides.

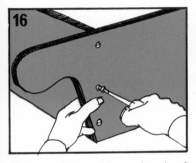

16

Screw and glue sides and ends of base box together. Use $1\frac{1}{2}$ in. No. 8 woodscrews.

17

Screw on casters to base box. Screws generally come with the casters when bought.

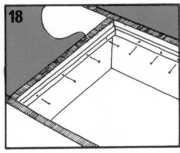

18

Tack thin timbers around top surface of smallest box to take dust lid.

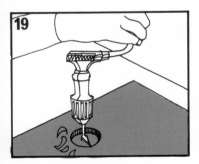

19

Drill 'finger holes' in lid. Start holes, reverse lid and complete from other side. This prevents splitting of ply.

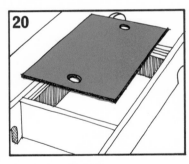

20

Check that the lid fits.

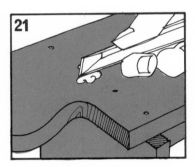

21

Fill in all holes, using wood filler.

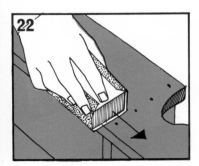

22

Sand down the filler flush with the surface.

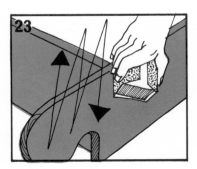

23

Sand down all edges.

24

Spray on paint, using lead free aerosol can paint. Alternatively, paint by hand.

Five-drawer Chest

The five-drawer chest uses a structure involving only the simplest jointing methods. The design incorporates a delicate balance of natural and painted finishes which can be varied according to personal taste and room decoration. It is primarily designed for storing clothes, although the size of drawer chosen makes it applicable for a variety of storage applications.

MATERIALS (in inches)					TOOLS	OTHER REQUIREMENTS
no. off	l.	w.	th.	description		
8	30	$1\frac{3}{4}$	$\frac{3}{4}$	outside framing	adjustable bevel	woodworking adhesive
30	17	$\frac{1}{2}$	$\frac{1}{2}$	drawer runners	brace and $\frac{1}{4}$ in. auger bit	polyurethane paint and varnish
10	24	$\frac{3}{8}$	$\frac{3}{8}$	drawer slips	screwdriver	2 in. brush
10	18	$\frac{3}{8}$	$\frac{3}{8}$	drawer slips	cork sanding block	glasspaper
10	24	$4\frac{1}{2}$	$\frac{1}{2}$	drawer fronts/backs	wheelbrace & drill bits	furniture wax
10	18	$4\frac{1}{2}$	$\frac{1}{2}$	drawer sides	back saw	1 in. No. 8 countersunk
2	24	5	$\frac{1}{2}$	false fronts	bench hook	woodscrews (36)
3	24	$4\frac{1}{2}$	$\frac{1}{2}$	false fronts	smoothing plane	pkg. 1 in. panel pins
5	$21\frac{1}{2}$	15	$\frac{3}{16}$	drawer bottoms	hammer	pkg. $\frac{3}{4}$ in. panels pins
2	$23\frac{1}{2}$	16	$\frac{1}{2}$	top and bottom	punch	
5	24	$1\frac{3}{4}$	$\frac{1}{2}$	handles	trysquare	

80

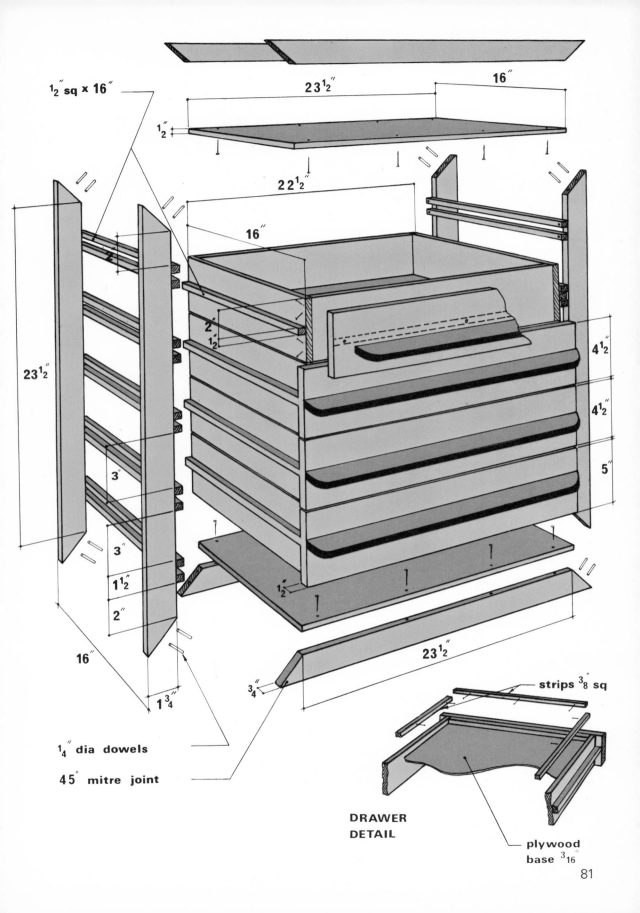

½" sq x 16"

23½"

16"

½"

22½"

16"

2"

½"

23½"

4½"

4½"

5"

3"

3"

1½"

2"

16"

1¾"

½"

¼" dia dowels

45° mitre joint

23½"

¾"

strips ⅜" sq

**DRAWER
DETAIL**

plywood
base ³⁄₁₆"

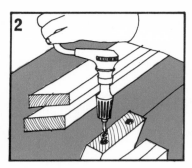

1 Mark out miters on outer frames, using an adjustable bevel set at 45°.

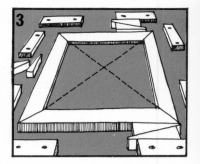

2 Mark positions of the dowels and drill the holes using brace and $\frac{1}{4}$ in. auger bit.

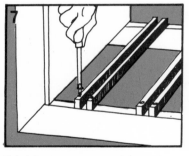

3 Glue frames together. Use a cramping board or sash cramps to apply pressure. Check for squareness.

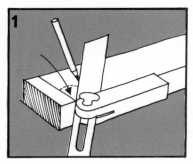

4 Sand down frames when glue is set.

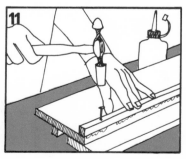

5 Paint top and base and screw to frames using 1 in. No. 8 woodscrews.

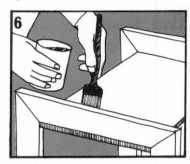

6 Varnish the frames with polyurethane varnish.

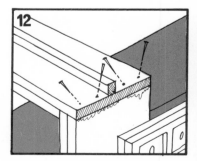

7 Paint drawer runners and screw to frames using 1 in. No. 8 woodscrews.

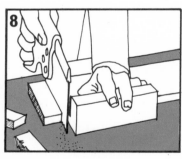

8 Saw drawer pieces to length, using back saw and bench hook.

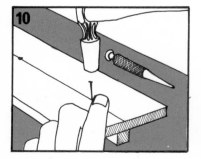

9 Plane end grain from each end to the center. Do not plane right across or wood will split.

10 Mark position, glue and tack drawer cleats on to sides of drawers using $\frac{3}{4}$ in. panel pins.

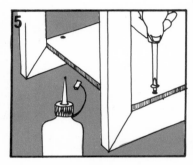

11 Glue and tack strips to take the drawer base.

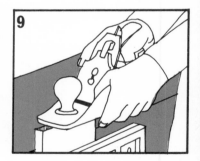

12 Assemble drawer. Glue and 'dovetail nail' the pieces together, using 1 in. panel pins.

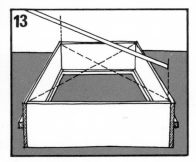

13

Check for squareness, using the 'diagonal test.'

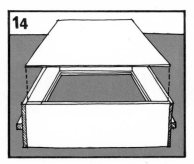

14

Cut the base to fit and glue and tack into position using $\frac{3}{4}$ in. panel pins.

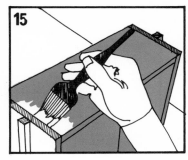

15

Check that drawer fits and then polyurethane varnish the finished drawer.

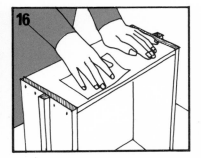

16

Sand down and apply a second coat of varnish.

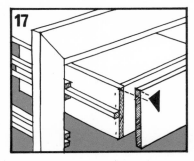

17

Note that false drawer-front is higher for top and bottom drawers.

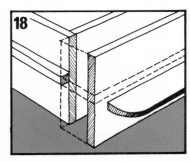

18

False drawer-front for center drawers is the same height as the drawers themselves.

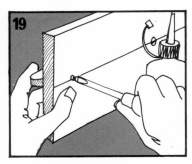

19

Paint handles and screw on to false drawer fronts using 1 in. No. 8 woodscrews.

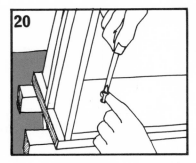

20

Screw false drawer fronts to the drawers. Use 2 in. No. 8 woodscrews.

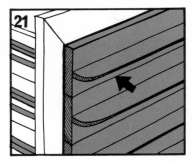

21

Check that drawers do not bind against one another. If they do, plane down the top edges carefully.

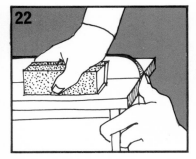

22

Sand down drawer-fronts, taking care not to mark painted handles.

23

Varnish drawer fronts.

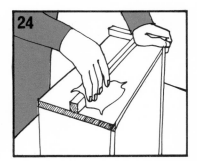

24

Wax drawer cleats on the sides of the drawers so that they run smoothly.

Bunk Beds

This is a design for single beds which will safely stack one on top of the other as bunk beds in rooms with limited space. The structure is robust and uncomplicated and the finished article represents a considerable saving in money.

MATERIALS (in inches)					TOOLS	OTHER REQUIREMENTS
no. off	l.	w.	th.	description		
8	36	$5\frac{1}{2}$	$\frac{3}{4}$	legs	back saw	woodworking adhesive
4	80	$5\frac{1}{2}$	$\frac{3}{4}$	side rails	bench hook	cardboard for template
4	40	$9\frac{1}{2}$	$\frac{3}{4}$	head boards	mortise gauge	fine sandpaper
4	33	$9\frac{1}{2}$	$\frac{3}{4}$	end rails	screwdriver	wedges
2	75	$32\frac{1}{2}$	$\frac{1}{2}$	mattress support	trysquare	masking tape
6	80	$\frac{3}{4}$	$\frac{3}{4}$	timbers	cork sanding block	2 in. No. 10 countersunk woodscrews (16)
1	48	$1\frac{3}{4}$	$1\frac{3}{4}$	blocks	coping saw	$1\frac{1}{4}$ in. No. 8 countersunk woodscrews (150)
3	40	$1\frac{1}{4}$	$1\frac{1}{4}$	ladder	$\frac{1}{2}$ in. mortise chisel	$1\frac{3}{4}$ in. No. 8 countersunk woodscrews (8)
2	75	$32\frac{1}{2}$	4	foam mattresses	rasp	polyurethane paint
					brace and straight-sided bit	

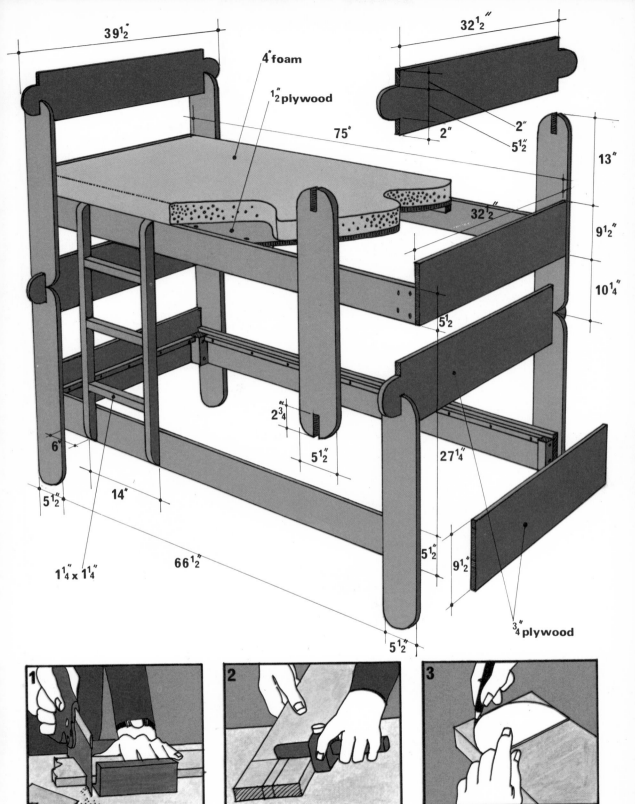

$39\frac{1}{2}"$

4" foam

$32\frac{1}{2}"$

$\frac{1}{2}"$ plywood

75"

2"

2"

$5\frac{1}{2}$

13"

$32\frac{1}{2}$

$9\frac{1}{2}"$

$10\frac{1}{4}"$

$5\frac{1}{2}$

6"

$2\frac{3}{4}"$

$27\frac{1}{4}"$

$5\frac{1}{2}"$

$5\frac{1}{2}$

$5\frac{1}{2}$

14"

$9\frac{1}{2}"$

$1\frac{1}{4}" \times 1\frac{1}{4}"$

$66\frac{1}{2}"$

$\frac{3}{4}"$ plywood

$5\frac{1}{2}"$

1 Square the ends of all pieces of wood and mark out and cut to length using a back saw and bench hook.

2 Set a mortise gauge to $\frac{3}{4}$ in. and gauge centrally the slot at the top and bottom of each leg.

3 Cut a semi-circular template from cardboard, radius $2\frac{3}{4}$ in., and mark out the round at the end of each leg.

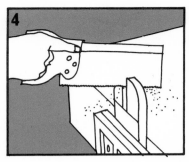

4

Cramp bed leg in vise and cut down to gauge lines; cut across grain with coping saw. Pare down to line with $\frac{1}{2}$ in. chisel.

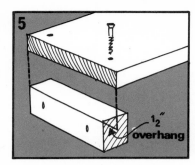

5

Screw and glue corner blocks to inside face of side rails, using 2 in. No. 10 woodscrews.

½" overhang

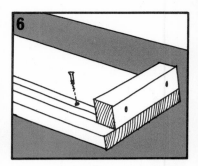

6

Screw and glue $\frac{7}{8}$ in. square timbers to inside faces of both side and end rails. Use $1\frac{1}{4}$ in. woodscrews.

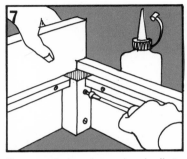

7

Screw and glue plywood end rails to side rails to complete the 2 bed frames. Use $1\frac{1}{4}$ in. woodscrews.

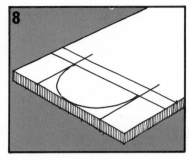

8

Mark out the end of each headboard rail, using the template and try-square.

9

Cut away waste wood with a back saw and coping saw.

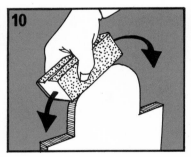

10

Sand down to the line with medium fine sandpaper wrapped firmly round a cork block.

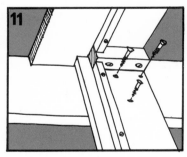

11

Screw and glue legs to main frame; make sure they are square to frame. Use $1\frac{1}{4}$ in. woodscrews.

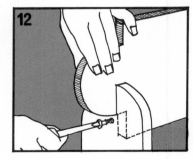

12

Screw and glue headboard to legs as illustrated. Use $1\frac{1}{4}$ in. woodscrews.

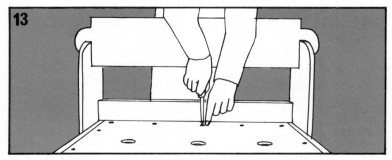

13

Drill out 1 in. holes in base at 8 in. intervals. Fit to main frame. Screw and glue, using $1\frac{1}{4}$ in. No. 8 screws.

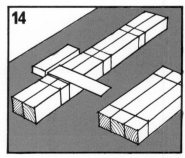

14

Cut ladder members to size and mark out mortise and tenon positions.

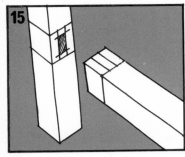

15 Set mortise gauge to $\frac{1}{2}$ in. mortise chisel and scribe position of all joints.

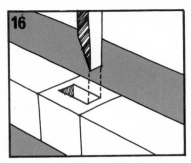

16 Cramp wood to the bench and chisel out mortises to a depth of 1 in.

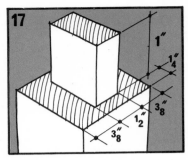

17 Cut tenons with back saw.

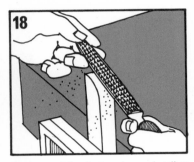

18 Cramp uprights in the vise and radius ends, using first a smoothing plane and then a rasp.

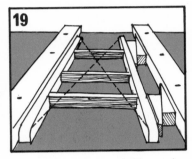

19 Glue and cramp up ladder, using blocks and wedges as illustrated. Check for squareness.

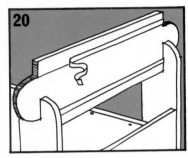

20 Sand down all wood and mask out with tape as shown. Apply painted finish.

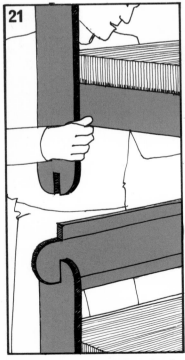

21 Fit one bed on top of the other by locating the cut-out on to headboard rail.

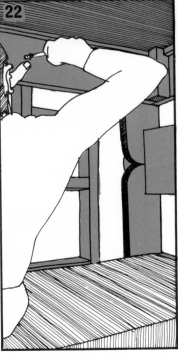

22 Screw the ladder into position from the inside, using $1\frac{3}{4}$ in. woodscrews.

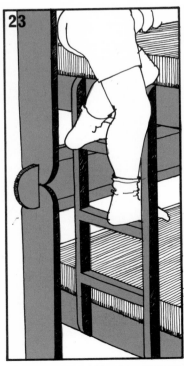

23 Mattresses should be 4 in. thick and covered in a suitable hardwearing material.

Hanging Space for Suits

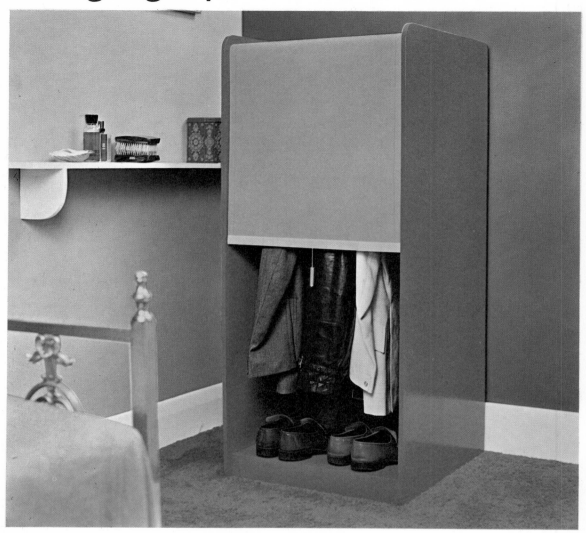

This unit provides an attractive colorful storage space for clothes and shoes. Dust is kept from the contents by using a roller blind, the color and/or pattern of which can be varied. The straightforward glue and screw assembly makes it easy to build and yet gives a robust structure.

MATERIALS (in inches)					TOOLS	OTHER REQUIREMENTS
no. off	l.	w.	th.	description		
2	48	24	$\frac{1}{2}$	sides	try-square	woodworking adhesive
1	48	20	$\frac{1}{8}$	back	back saw	$19\frac{3}{4}$ in. roller blind with 6 ft. 6 in.
1	20	20	$\frac{1}{2}$	bottom	bench hook	drop
4	22	$2\frac{3}{4}$	$\frac{3}{4}$	rails	G-cramps	masking tape
2	22	$1\frac{3}{8}$	$\frac{3}{4}$	rails	screwdriver	polyurethane paint
2	22	$\frac{3}{4}$	$\frac{3}{4}$	timbers	$\frac{1}{2}$ in. beveled edge chisel	pkg. panel pins
2	48	$\frac{7}{8}$	$\frac{3}{8}$	strips	smoothing plane	fine sandpaper
1	22	1	dia.	dowel	wheelbrace and drill bits	2 in. paint brush
1	48	$\frac{1}{4}$	dia.	dowel	pliers	1 in. No. 8 countersunk
					pincers	woodscrews (12)
					brace and $\frac{1}{4}$ in. auger	standard wood filler
					compass	
					cork sanding block	

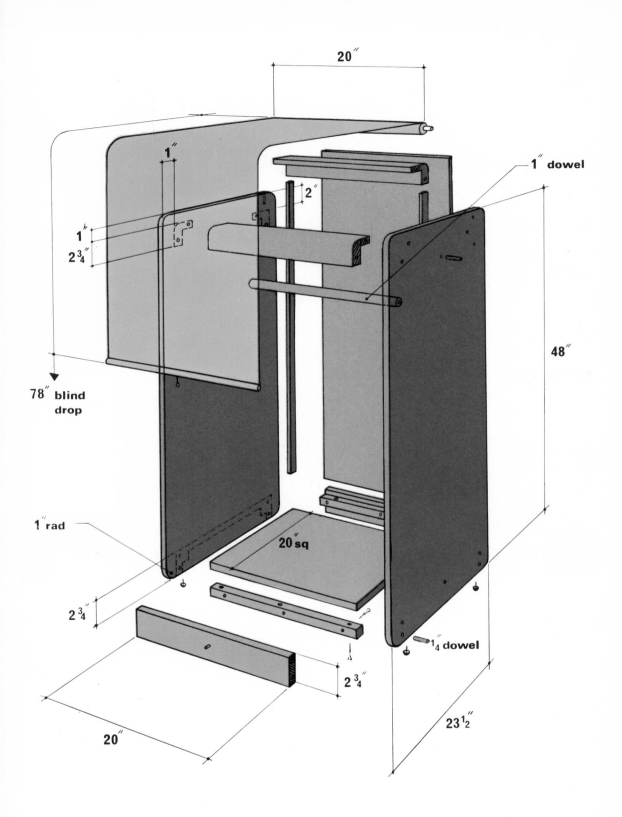

20"

1"

1"

2"

1"

2 3/4"

1" dowel

78" blind
drop

48"

1" rad

20 sq

2 3/4"

1 1/4" dowel

2 3/4"

20"

23 1/2"

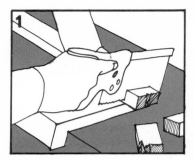

Check width of roller blind; cut cross-rails to the same width using back saw and bench hook.

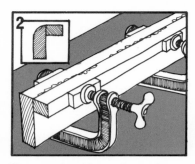

Glue together pieces that make up top cross-rails. G-cramp pieces together. When dry chamfer top edge as shown in small insert.

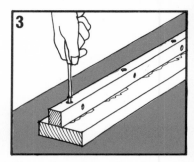

Glue and screw together pieces that make up bottom cross-rails. Use 1 in. No. 8 woodscrews.

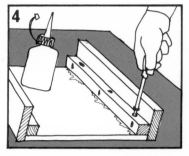

Screw wardrobe base to bottom cross-rails, using 1 in. woodscrews.

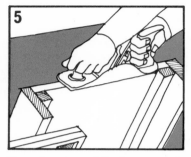

Plane the edges of the base smooth and square.

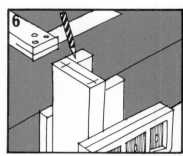

Mark out dowel positions in the top and bottom rails, using a trysquare.

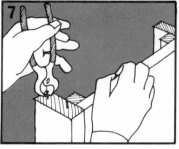

Tap in panel pins to mark these positions. Clip off pin heads with pliers.

Mark position of base and top rails on the sides by pressing the pins into the sides.

Drill the dowel holes.

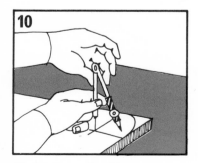

Mark radius on the sides.

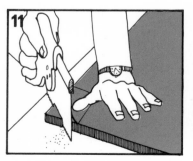

Saw out rough profile of the radius using back saw.

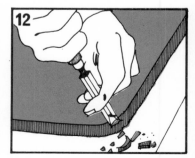

Chisel down to the scribed radius, using beveled edge chisel.

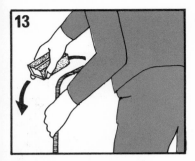

13

Sand down radius and edges of the plywood sides using sandpaper over cork block.

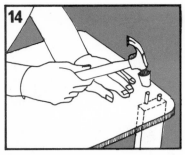

14

Dowel sides to top rails and the base unit.

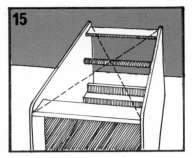

15

Check for squareness, using the 'diagonal test.'

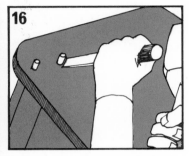

16

Chisel off any remaining dowel.

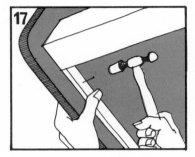

17

Pin battens to sides in readiness for the wardrobe back.

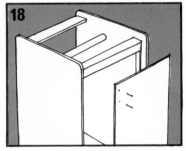

18

Pin the back into position.

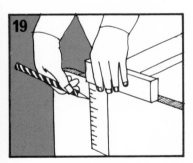

19

Mark the position of the roller blind. (The fittings provided with the blind are not required.)

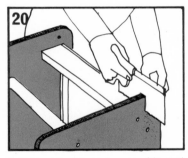

20

Drill the blind hole in one side and saw a slot in the other using a back saw.

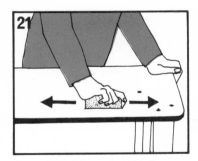

21

Fill and sand down dowel holes.

22

Paint the whole of the wardrobe and then mask off and paint side panels if a different color is required.

23

Fit the roller blind.

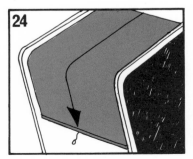

24

Check that the motion of the roller blind is satisfactory.

Toy Soldier and Queen

An arrangement of large, circular pieces of wood which are shaped, painted and decorated make up the parts of these toys. By juggling with the position or size of the pieces it is possible to make up a tall or short figure and vary its appearance. Turned wood of the required diameter can be bought directly from a lumber yard.

MATERIALS (in inches)					TOOLS	OTHER REQUIREMENTS
no. off	l.	w.	th.	description		
1	30	$2\frac{1}{2}$	dia.	toy bodies	back saw	woodworking adhesive
1	6	$\frac{1}{2}$	dia.	dowel	smoothing plane	balsa cement
					brace and $\frac{1}{2}$ in. auger bit	colored paper
					$\frac{1}{2}$ in. and $\frac{3}{4}$ in. beveled edge chisel	acrylic paints
					No. 3, 6 & 10 paint brushes	bristles
					tweezers	feathers
						silver paper
						sequins etc.

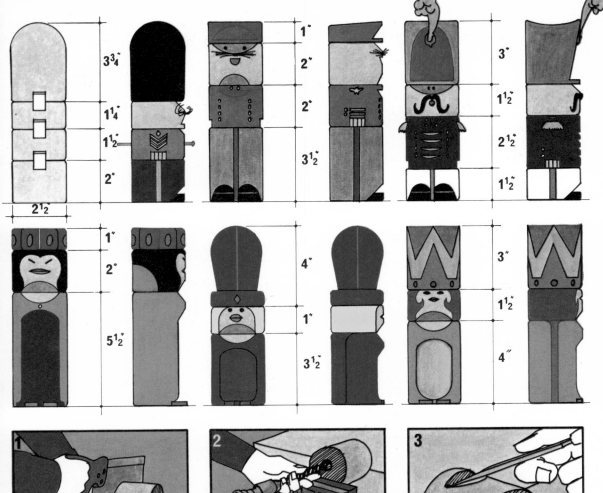

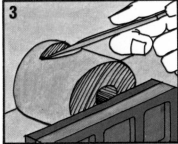

1
Mark out lengths of each of the parts that make up toy. Cut with back saw. Square off both ends with smoothing plane.

2
Mark out dowel position. Drill to depth of $\frac{1}{2}$ in. using a brace and $\frac{1}{2}$ in. auger. Glue dowels on to upper faces.

3
Make cut with tenon saw and chisel down to depth of cut. A variety of forms can be achieved in this way.

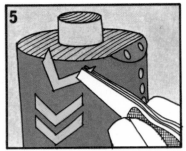

4
Oddments can be used to decorate the toys. Bristles from a broom make an ideal mustache as illustrated.

5
A wide variety of colored papers can be used to cut out epaulettes, medals, stripes, etc. These must be carefully glued.

6
The main body of the toy can be painted with acrylic colors. These paints dilute with water and dry quickly.

Candlestick

A decorative spiral of identical triangular pieces of wood mounted vertically on a central dowel and displaced 10 degrees from each other. Any hardwood can be used and choice will probably depend on color preference. It can be used for ornamental purposes or on the table at dinner parties. The finished article should be polyurethane varnished or painted.

MATERIALS (in inches)					TOOLS	OTHER REQUIREMENTS
no. off	l.	w.	th.	description		
1	120	3	$\frac{3}{16}$	triangles	tenon saw	cardboard for template
1	24	$\frac{3}{8}$	dia.	dowel	brace and $\frac{3}{8}$ in. auger bit	polurethane varnish or paint
1	6	$1\frac{1}{2}$	$\frac{7}{8}$	top pieces	$\frac{3}{4}$ in. beveled edge chisel	woodworking adhesive
					adjustable bevel	fine sandpaper
					pliers	package of panel pins